30 AND UNWRITTEN

From Heartbreak to Healing
A Story Still Unfolding

PANKHURI JAIN

INDIA • SINGAPORE • MALAYSIA

ISBN
Paperback 979-8-89724-542-0
Hardcase 979-8-89744-898-2

To my beloved Shivam,

You may not be here, but your love is woven into every page of this book. You taught me love, strength, and the courage to keep going.

And to my dearest Shivankh,

You are my reason, my hope, my greatest blessing. Every lesson in this book is something I hope you one day understand.

This book is for both of you—with all my heart.

A Note to Readers

While this book draws from real-life experiences, some names and identifying details have been changed to protect the privacy of individuals. This story is a personal reflection on my journey and the events that have shaped my life. It is not intended to point fingers or assign blame. These instances are integral to my narrative, and excluding them would compromise the authenticity of my story. If any resemblance to actual persons, living or deceased, is unintentional or causes hurt, please accept my sincerest apologies.

Contents

Preface

I never imagined I'd be telling my story this way. Life wasn't supposed to unfold like this—not with love cut short, dreams left incomplete, and a path I never chose but was forced to walk. And yet, here I am, writing these words, not as someone who has all the answers, but as someone who has learned—sometimes the hard way—that even in the darkest moments, life leaves us with lessons, some painful, some beautiful, but all essential.

When I turned 30, it wasn't the milestone I had once envisioned. It wasn't a grand celebration of achievements or a moment to check off the boxes of societal success. Instead, it was a reckoning—a quiet confrontation with everything I had lost, everything I had endured, and everything I had become. In that moment, I realized that while my journey had been filled with pain, it had also been a testament to resilience, love, and growth.

This book isn't just about grief or survival; it's about transformation. It's about the lessons life teaches us—sometimes gently, sometimes through heart-wrenching experiences. Each chapter reflects a truth I've come to understand, whether through love, loss, friendships, or the simple, everyday moments that shape us in ways we don't always recognize.

I share these lessons not because I have mastered them, but because I am still learning—still growing, still healing. My hope is that in these pages, you find echoes of your own struggles and triumphs, reminders that you are not alone, and, most importantly, the courage to embrace your own journey with grace.

Life is unpredictable. It doesn't always give us what we want, but it always gives us what we need to grow. This book is my attempt to honor that growth—to turn my experiences into words that might offer comfort, reflection, or perhaps even a guiding light for someone else.

So, as you read, I invite you to not just see my story, but to reflect on your own. May these lessons remind you to cherish what you have, to set boundaries, to heal, to love deeply, and most of all—to keep going. Because no matter what life throws at us, we always have the power to rise.

With love and strength,

Pankhuri

Introduction

Ah, 30. Not exactly the birthday most people dream of, but for me, it wasn't as gloomy as you might think. Why? Well, to understand that, let's rewind a bit...

Flashback: June 13th, 2021

Just eight days after bringing our son, Shivankh, home from the hospital, our house was buzzing. Relatives and friends poured in to meet the newest member of the family. The living room felt like a scene from a family movie—people chatting, passing around trays of sweets, and clicking pictures with Cheeku (as we fondly called Shivankh). It was chaos, but the kind that warms your heart.

Except for Shivam.

While everyone else enjoyed the happy commotion, my husband was on a mission: Operation Maximum Sleep for Baby Shivankh. Every loud laugh or clink of a teacup made him twitch. He'd hush people, adjust the curtains to block out light, and hover near the baby's crib like a protective force field.

It was amusing to see this carefree guy—who once slept through firecracker-filled Diwalis—transform into a hyper-aware dad overnight. But honestly, it melted my heart. Watching him care so deeply for our little Cheeku made me feel like everything I'd ever dreamed of was right here, under one roof. My family felt complete. Perfect.

But perfection, as I was about to learn, can be fleeting.

That afternoon, Shivam and I lay on the bed, with tiny, swaddled Cheeku sleeping between us. We talked softly, weaving dreams about our future. Trips to Goa, me getting back into shape, Cheeku's schooling—it felt like the beginning of our happily ever after.

"I feel so lucky to have you," I told him, my voice barely above a whisper. "Thank you for everything, Shivam. For being the kind, loving man you are."

He smiled at me, brushing a strand of hair off my face. "I should be thanking you, Pankhu. For always believing in me, even when I didn't deserve it."

Shivam and I were college sweethearts. We'd been together for five years before tying the knot in 2019. We avoided the usual drama that comes with love marriages in India, but life had thrown us our own share of challenges. And now, here we were, holding our little piece of heaven—everything we'd ever wanted, finally ours.

But life doesn't pause for perfect moments.

In the days following Shivankh's arrival, all Shivam wanted was to be home with us. His friends, however, insisted on a celebratory night out. After a couple of polite declines, he reluctantly agreed.

That night, around 10 p.m., my phone buzzed. Eight missed calls from Shivam.

My heart raced as I unlocked the screen. I'd kept the phone on silent to avoid disturbing Cheeku, and now panic set in. What had happened?

I called him back immediately.

"Hello?" I blurted out. "What happened? Is everything okay?"

"Arey baba, calm down," he replied, his voice calm and reassuring. "Why are you panicking?"

"You called me eight times!" I said, my voice trembling. "Papa ji told me to keep the phone on silent so Cheeku wouldn't wake up, but now I'm worried. Is everything alright?"

He chuckled softly and said, "Oh, my dear Pankhu, why do you worry so much? Nothing bad is going to happen, not anymore, and why should you worry when I'm here? In fact, I'm sorry I got so late, but I wanted Bhaiya to have fun too, so I invited him. He joined late, but now only dinner is left. Honestly, I'm planning to skip it—I just can't wait to be with both of you again."

I let out a shaky laugh. "Wow, what a change! Cheeku has done in seven days what I couldn't do in seven years—get you to leave your friends early."

He laughed again. "I know, I know. I haven't always been my best, but these past few days made me realize something. I can't live without you. And now we have Cheeku. I've decided—I'm going to become my best version for both of you."

I smiled, tears stinging my eyes. "Alright, mister 'best version.' Stay, have dinner, and then come home safely. We have our whole lives to talk and plan, okay?"

"Okay, my lord," he teased. "What's Cheeku doing?"

"Sleeping," I replied. "I'll wake him up when you get back so you can play with him for a bit."

"Perfect. I'll be there soon," he said. "And Pankhu?"

"Yes?"

"I love you. So, so much."

I laughed. "I love you too. Now go eat something and come back to me."

"Just give me 15 minutes," he said.

"No 15 minutes," I insisted. "Drive slowly. Park the bike there and come back by car with Bhaiya."

"Okay, my lord," he said with a smile in his voice. And then the call ended.

I didn't know it would be the last time I'd hear his voice.

By 10:15 p.m., everything changed.

A tragic accident took Shivam away from us forever.

He was just 26. I was 27. And our baby, barely eight days old, was left without a father.

It felt like the world shattered around me, leaving an emptiness so vast that it seemed impossible to breathe.

Life Goes On, But Not Quite

Life, of course, didn't have the courtesy to stop.

Shivankh grew, blissfully unaware of the gaping hole in our lives. His giggles filled the silence that had settled over our home, a bittersweet reminder that life goes on, even when your heart feels shattered.

These past three years, from the age of 27 to 30, have felt like an eternity. Each passing year brings me closer to the day when my son won't need me as desperately. It makes living feel...compulsory, not joyful.

But my story isn't just about grief. Turning 30 has made me look back at my entire life. These past three years have been a crash course in life lessons, lessons learned from the people around me and from my own experiences. But, as you'll see, some of these lessons came a little too late.

This is where my story truly begins. A story of love, loss, and the life lessons that have shaped me.

Buckle up as I share the 30 lessons life has taught me—lessons learned, yes, but often learned a little too late.

Lesson 01

The Rebirth of Self-Love

It was 31st March 2024, and I was sitting in a salon with my three-year-old son, Cheeku, wriggling on my lap, his tiny fingers tugging playfully at my hair. Mom sat nearby in her simple cotton suit, chatting politely with the stylist. Her presence was steady and warm, but her calm demeanor was in sharp contrast to the storm of emotions brewing within me.

"Cheeku, sit still, baby," I said, trying to keep him entertained.

"But sitting is boring, Mumma!" he replied, his mischievous smile making me laugh despite myself.

I smiled at him, but my mind was elsewhere. This wasn't just another birthday—it was my 30th. A milestone. And as much as I wanted to feel excitement, I couldn't ignore the weight of everything this day symbolized. My life, my choices, my losses—they all played like a movie in my mind, frame by frame.

Soon, the day would turn lively. My brother-in-law and sister-in-law were joining soon for the celebration. The usual suspects—my family, my pillars of strength—were coming too. When I say "my family," it's never just my parents, Cheeku, or my brother. It includes my maternal side: Chhote Mama, Chhoti Mami, Yash, and Yashi. These people are the ones who shaped me—sometimes lovingly, sometimes through heated arguments and misunderstandings—but always standing by me when it truly mattered.

This was my 30th birthday. Thirty years of life, thirty times this day had come and gone. But this year, it felt different. Something was stirring inside me, though I didn't know exactly what it was at the time. Maybe it was the reflection of everything I had gone through in the past few years—the ups, the downs, the losses, the lessons—that made this birthday feel like more than just another date.

Before Shivam came into my life, birthdays were magical. My parents went all out—gifts, pampering sessions at the salon, grand parties. I was their princess, and they made sure the world knew it. Even after Shivam entered my life, he had matched their enthusiasm. He understood how much birthdays meant to me, how I started planning them as soon as the New Year began.

But after marriage, things changed. My first birthday as a married woman coincided with the Covid-19 lockdown. I didn't expect a grand celebration, but a small gesture—a cake, flowers, or even a heartfelt song—would have made all the difference. Instead, it felt like any other day.

"Maybe we'll do something once the lockdown eases," Shivam had said casually.

"But even something small, Shivam, just us... wouldn't that be nice?" I had hinted, trying to keep the lump in my throat from turning into tears.

But nothing came of it. His family's culture was different—they didn't prioritize such celebrations. While my niece, nephew, and sister-in-law tried their best to make me feel special, the void was undeniable. For the first time, Shivam hadn't met my expectations, and I couldn't hide my disappointment. That day ended in arguments and tears. It was the first time I began to question whether I had expected too much—or if I had compromised too much.

I know some people reading this might judge me. They might think, Even now, when Shivam isn't here, she's complaining. But this isn't a complaint. It's a wound—one that no matter how much I try to erase, still feels fresh.

A year later, things seemed to improve slightly. By then, I was seven months pregnant. Shivam still didn't like celebrating Valentine's Day, but I did. That February, I watched couples in our building, friends, and even strangers on the street, dressed up and celebrating. I felt a pang of longing. I, too, had always wanted those moments. But my love for Shivam had always been greater than my desire for such occasions, so I learned to live his way.

When Shivam told me he was planning something special for my birthday that year, I felt a flicker of excitement. Maybe this time would be different. But fate had other plans. Just before my birthday, we traveled for his brother's roka ceremony, which I was genuinely excited about. But then, the unexpected happened—again.

On my birthday, his mom announced that Shivam needed to accompany them for jewelry shopping for my sister-in-law. I was stunned. I couldn't hold back my tears and went straight to my room. Shivam saw me and tried to convince them to change the dates or excuse him, but it wasn't possible for several reasons. I could see him getting sandwiched between me and his family, but the pain of seeing my life change so much, of facing disappointment after disappointment, was too much to bear.

Finally, Shivam managed to convince them that I should accompany him. "At least we'll be together," he said, trying to console me. But the day had already lost its meaning.

Seventeen days after my birthday, it was our anniversary—a day I had always cherished and looked forward to. But as the morning sun streamed through the curtains, I woke up to find Shivam gone. On the bedside table was a hastily scribbled note: "Had to leave for some urgent work. Sorry."

I stared at the note, the words blurring as tears welled up in my eyes. This is it, I thought. The weight of disappointment settled on my chest like a heavy stone. It wasn't just the note, or the fact that he had left without even waiting to share a moment together—it was the pattern. The missed gestures, the overlooked emotions, the small cracks in the foundation of our relationship that were growing deeper with each passing milestone.

I sat on the edge of the bed, the silence of the house pressing down on me. For the first time, I let myself ask a question I had been avoiding: Was marrying Shivam a mistake? I had always believed love would conquer everything, but now I wasn't so sure. Maybe I had rushed into marriage without truly understanding his background, his values, his approach to life.

That noon, the house was quiet. I sat down at my desk, took out a sheet of paper, and began to write. I didn't know where to start, so I let the words flow straight from my heart.

"Shivam," I began, "I can't keep doing this to myself. I've decided that from now on, I will never celebrate any milestone in our life—except for our child's birthdays. No anniversaries, no birthdays, no special days. I don't want to keep expecting something that won't happen. I can't keep feeling this hurt over and over again."

Tears stained the paper as I wrote, but I didn't stop. I told him how much I loved him, but also how much it hurt to feel invisible, to have my feelings dismissed time and again. I wasn't angry; I was tired. Tired of hoping, tired of wishing, tired of waiting.

As I folded the letter, I felt a strange sense of calm. It wasn't the calm of resolution—it was the calm of surrender. I told myself I was becoming "mature," learning to lower my expectations and accept the reality of our life together. I believed I was protecting myself from further disappointment by building a wall around my heart.

Little did I know that those words would come true in the most devastating way. I would never get another chance to celebrate 17th April with Shivam. That was it.

By the time my next birthday came around in 2022, I had lost all excitement for the day. The girl who used to start planning her birthdays months in advance, dreaming of cakes, parties, and gifts, was gone. I didn't want to see anyone or speak to anyone. The day felt like a burden—a painful reminder of everything I had lost, not just Shivam but also a part of myself.

For two years, I refused to celebrate. I didn't cut a cake or invite anyone over. I told myself I didn't care, that birthdays didn't matter anymore. But deep down, the pain lingered. I wasn't avoiding celebrations because I had moved on—I was avoiding them because I couldn't bear the weight of my own disappointment.

This year, something shifted. It wasn't a grand epiphany or a sudden realization. It was a quiet feeling, a spark that slowly grew into a flame. For the first time in years, I felt like celebrating my birthday again—not for others, not for appearances, but for me.

I didn't fully understand why at first. But as the days passed, I began to see the truth. Those two years of silence, of refusing to celebrate, had been a time of healing. In that quiet, I had begun to unravel the deepest truths about myself.

I realized that I had spent my entire life waiting for others to make me happy. I had always looked to my parents, Shivam, or my friends to make me feel special, to validate my worth. But I had never done that for myself. A sentence someone once told me came back to me: "You should learn to enjoy your own company." And then, my therapist's words echoed in my mind: "Have you ever experienced unconditional love? Do you love yourself unconditionally?"

The answer, I realized, had always been no. I had sought love, validation, and happiness from others—never from within. I had compromised my dreams, my career, my sense of self, all because I believed I had to. I thought that to be loved, I needed to change.

As I reflected on the years I had spent with Shivam, a difficult question haunted me: *Why didn't I say no to the things I was not comfortable with?* I kept asking myself that over and over. What would have happened if I had? Either he would have left me, or he would have married me exactly as I was—with all my desires, my quirks, my boundaries, my dreams. But I didn't give myself that chance.

The truth was painful to admit, but it was clear: I didn't say no because I doubted my worth. Deep down, I believed I wasn't worthy of being loved unconditionally, without compromise. I thought I had to change pieces of myself—sometimes small, sometimes significant—to make others happy, to fit into their expectations. And because I doubted myself, I didn't even realize that I had stopped loving myself.

That realization hit hard. It wasn't just about Shivam; it was about me. I had compromised on so many things—not because I had to, but because I thought that's what love required. Living in a place I didn't want to, not prioritizing my career, changing my style, adjusting my entire identity—I did all of that because I thought that's what it took to be loved.

But now, after years of healing, I see the truth. I loved Shivam deeply, and I know he loved me too. Standing up for myself, raising my voice, or refusing something I wasn't comfortable with wouldn't have meant I loved him any less. And if someone couldn't see that—if they couldn't see my pain or respect my perspective—then they weren't truly mine.

For the first time, I realized I was no less beautiful, no less special, no less worthy of love than anyone else. That's why Shivam had loved me in the first place—because of who I was. Not because of the compromises I made. I see now that I didn't need to change to deserve love.

Even though Shivam isn't here anymore, and life feels so different without him, I have clarity about one thing: even when he was with me, we didn't always celebrate everything. And before he came into my life, I celebrated fully and joyfully. So why should anything stop me now?

This year, I understood something profound: this is my life. This is my birthday. And I deserve to celebrate it—not for anyone else, not for appearances, but for me. I deserve to feel special, happy, and whole, simply because I exist.

At 30, I learned that loving myself doesn't mean I love others any less—it simply means I finally see my own worth. And from that place of strength, I can choose who matters in my life and who doesn't. I don't need to seek validation from anyone anymore because I know my own value.

That's why this birthday wasn't just another day—it was my rebirth. A new Pankhuri was born. One who cares for her self-esteem, her choices, and her happiness. One who knows she is worthy of love, just as she is.

This year, I celebrated my birthday as if I was being born again—a new Pankhuri, one who loved herself fiercely and unapologetically. For the first time in years, I cut a cake with joy in my heart. The room was filled with warmth and laughter, not because someone else made the day special, but because I chose to make it special for myself.

At 30, I learned that I didn't need anyone else to validate my worth or happiness. Loving myself didn't mean I loved others any less—it simply meant I was finally treating myself with the same care and respect I had always given to everyone else.

The Lesson

So here's the lesson I learned: You are enough, just as you are. You are worth celebrating—not because of what you do for others, but because you exist. Love yourself unapologetically, and every day becomes a celebration.

That's how this birthday became my rebirth—the birth of a new Pankhuri, one who finally chose me.

A Simple Exercise for Reflection

Step 1: Reflect on Compromises (10 minutes)

- Take a journal or a piece of paper and divide it into two columns.
- In the **first column**, list all the things you've compromised on in your life—big or small. Examples: decisions about where to live, career choices, how you express yourself, hobbies you let go of, or traditions you stopped celebrating.
- In the **second column**, write *why* you compromised. Be honest. Was it to keep peace, to avoid conflict, to meet others' expectations, or because you doubted your right to say no?
- Look at your list. How many of these compromises came from a place of love for others versus a fear of being unworthy of love?

Step 2: Revisit Your Authentic Self (10 minutes)

- Close your eyes and take a few deep breaths. Picture yourself before these compromises—before you believed you needed to change to be loved.
- Ask yourself:
  - What did I love about myself back then?
  - What did I enjoy doing that I no longer do?
  - What dreams, goals, or traditions brought me joy?
- Write about this version of yourself. Describe them in detail—their personality, dreams, quirks, and strengths. What makes them lovable? How can you reconnect with this version of yourself today?

Step 3: Reclaim Your Worth (10 minutes)

Write a letter to yourself as if you were a friend or mentor, reminding yourself of your worth. Include affirmations such as:

- "I am worthy of love just as I am."
- "My boundaries are valid, and honoring them doesn't make me unloving—it makes me strong."
- "I deserve to celebrate myself and my life, not for others, but for me."

End the letter by listing three small ways you can honor yourself starting today.

Lesson 02

The Gift of Now

Growing up, we hear it time and again: Don't take things for granted. Appreciate what you have. It's the kind of wisdom that gets lost in the background noise of childhood, lumped in with reminders to clean our rooms or finish our vegetables. Back then, it felt like just another thing adults said—something we nodded along to without really understanding.

I was no exception. And honestly, neither was Shivam. Like most couples, we were dreamers. From the moment we decided to spend our lives together, we painted a vision of our future: a cozy apartment in the city, fulfilling careers, and a life that wasn't extravagant but felt perfect for us. We were so focused on building that future that we often forgot to pause and live in the now.

Life after college wasn't smooth. There was the rush of graduation, the stress of job hunting, and the delicate balancing act of maintaining a relationship. At first, marriage wasn't even on our radar. But life has a funny way of rewriting your plans. Curveballs kept coming, forcing us to adapt, regroup, and make decisions we hadn't prepared for.

Suddenly, we were engaged, planning a wedding, then postponing it, all while trying to launch our careers and fulfill family expectations. It was chaos, which became our new normal. But amidst all the noise, there was one constant: Shivam. His presence was my anchor, and I like to think I was his. Even when we were overwhelmed, we found solace in the fact that we had each other.

By 2019, we finally said "I do." But married life didn't begin the way we had envisioned. Our dreams of living in a specific city and pursuing certain career paths quickly unraveled. Circumstances beyond our control brought us to Shivam's hometown instead, a place that demanded sacrifices neither of us were prepared for. For me, it meant putting my career on hold and adapting to a more conservative lifestyle—a stark contrast to the life I had imagined.

We argued more than ever during those years. Small disagreements turned into bitter fights, and the weight of unmet dreams often felt like it would crush us. Yet, through it all, we never wavered in one thing: our commitment to each other. No matter how frustrated or disheartened we were, our hearts never stopped wanting the same thing—to be happy together. We learned to hold on, even when life felt like it was pulling us apart.

There were moments of joy amidst the chaos, quiet times that reminded us why we chose each other. After an argument, we would go on long, silent walks, holding hands but saying nothing. Deep down, we both knew the fights weren't about us; they were about the circumstances we were battling together. Those walks weren't just a truce—they were a reminder that even when life didn't go as planned, we still had each other.

Looking back, those years weren't perfect, but they were beautiful in their own way. Our love didn't just survive those challenges; it grew stronger. But there was one thing I wish I had done more often: said the words. I always believed that my actions spoke louder than words, that Shivam didn't need constant reminders of how much I loved him. I thought he just knew.

June 13th, 2021

Everything changed on June 13th, 2021. I don't know why, but that day, an overwhelming urge consumed me to tell Shivam how much he meant to me. I wanted him to know how lucky I felt to be his wife, how deeply I loved him. And for once, I didn't hold back. I said it all, every word I had held inside for too long.

Now, when I think about that day, I'm filled with equal parts gratitude and heartbreak. Gratitude because I got to tell him how I felt. Heartbreak because it was one of the last times I had the chance to do so. The thought of not expressing my love that day chills me to the core. It's a regret I couldn't have borne.

Even though I cherish those memories, one regret lingers. While we did our best to live in the moment and appreciate each other, there were times when the weight of unmet expectations dulled our happiness. We were disheartened by how far our reality was from the life we had dreamed of. And in trying so hard to reshape our future, we sometimes forgot to fully embrace the beauty of our present.

Today, I have everything we once planned for: a city apartment, a thriving career, the occasional luxury vacation, and, most importantly, our little one, Shivankh. But Shivam isn't here to share it with me. Without him, these achievements feel hollow. I often find myself looking back at those imperfect days in his hometown and realizing that, despite everything, those were some of the happiest moments of my life—because we had each other.

The Lesson

This journey has taught me a lesson I can't emphasize enough: never postpone love, gratitude, or appreciation. Don't wait for the "right time" to tell someone how much they mean to you. Cherish what you have, now, because tomorrow is never guaranteed. Life can change in an instant, and the only thing worse than loss is living with the "what ifs" of things unsaid.

So today, and every day, I tell the people I love how much they mean to me. I don't assume they know—I say it out loud, again and again. I savor the small moments, the everyday miracles, because they are the true gifts of life. And I hope, as you read this, you're reminded to do the same. Hold your loved ones close, tell them how you feel, and live fully in this moment—because it's the only one we truly have.

A Simple Exercise for Reflection

Consider three individuals who have profoundly impacted your life. Write each of them a heartfelt letter or message, expressing your gratitude and love. Be specific about what they mean to you and how they have influenced your life.

Lesson 03

Words That Heal, Words That Harm

Grief is a lonely island. It's a place where words can either be a lifeline or a weapon. In those first excruciating days after Shivam's accident, I experienced both sides of that coin.

It had been just two or three days since Shivam was torn away from me, and the raw ache of loss gripped my throat, stealing my voice. My room was filled with people—some I'd never met before and others I saw every day but was seeing their true selves for the first time. While the fog of those early days blurs most memories, certain moments stand out in horrifying detail, like shards of broken glass lodged in my heart. I remember the whispers about my age. "She is so young," they'd say, their pity cutting me like a knife. "How will she manage on her own?" they'd ask, a question that echoed in the emptiness of my chest. "Maybe she should think about remarrying," some suggested, as if offering a life raft to someone drowning in a stormy sea.

But added that it would be difficult with a child, advising me to leave my son with my in-laws. Others blamed our fate, questioning if we had matched kundlis before marriage. One person shared how they couldn't imagine a day without their husband and couldn't fathom how I would live the rest of my life alone. Then there were those who simply wanted to video call and see how I was holding up, while others spoke about the dangers of being a single parent and the negative impact it could have on my child.

All these words just kept pouring in, and I was left trying to find answers to questions I never wanted to face. It felt like my problems would never end.

Amidst all this noise, there were a few who were my anchors. They didn't say much; they just fed me and stood by my side, taking care of my son when I couldn't. Their presence was like a balm to my soul. They didn't offer advice or ask questions—they were just there, and that made all the difference.

And then there were my friends. They didn't come with big advice or grand gestures; instead, they carried me through with simple words that became my lifeline. "I know you can do it; take it one day at a time." "We know it's not easy, but we know you—you will do good, you are doing good." "Keep moving; we are here to have your back." They didn't realize how meeting them, hearing those words, and having those small conversations gave me the strength to push mountains every time I started losing faith in myself.

I'm not sharing this to point fingers at those who spoke carelessly, but to express the pain I felt listening to those words when I was already struggling to breathe, to live, so my son wouldn't lose his second parent too. Those words echoed in my mind for months, haunting my nights, until a time which I'll discuss later in this book.

The Lesson

From this, I learned another lesson: the importance of knowing what to say in certain situations. If you're unsure of your words, it's better to stay silent. Even the right words, said at the wrong time, can feel like poison. You can imagine how much worse it is to hear the wrong words during such a difficult time.

A Simple Exercise for Reflection

Think about it:

Have you ever received words that cut deep, or lifted you up?

Have you ever comforted someone by simply being there?

Lesson 04

Your Circle Shapes You

This lesson applies to both my younger and adult life. As a teenager, I was a bit on the heavier side. This affected my confidence, making me withdraw from social circles. However, at that time, all I cared about was growth – my career, my future.

In high school, I was just...average. Average in looks, studies, social life. My self-esteem was rock bottom, and I believed I wasn't good enough to have real connections.

I think my weight-related insecurities made me so withdrawn that I lost interest in socializing. Teenagers, on the other hand, are often preoccupied with crushes and relationships, and I just wasn't part of that scene. It wasn't because people were necessarily mean; I just felt invisible...why? Because -

a. My weight made me feel so inadequate that I preferred being alone.

b. There was no one around to point out my positive traits or celebrate my achievements. It felt like I just blended into the background, unnoticed and unappreciated.

Then came college, and everything shifted.

On my very first day, I took a deep breath, swallowed my fear, and introduced myself to the class:

"Hi, I'm Pankhuri Jain. I studied at Laurels School International, Indore. Honestly, BBA isn't my first choice—I've always wanted to study psychology. While I couldn't pursue it right now, I plan to in the future. For now, I'm focusing on HR so I can incorporate psychology into my learning."

What happened next blew my mind. People responded with smiles, admiration, and genuine curiosity. My classmates and even the teacher were impressed. Suddenly, I wasn't invisible anymore. Everyone wanted to talk to me, hang out with me. That one moment of validation? It changed everything. It felt like someone had flipped a switch inside me.

I stopped hiding. I started taking initiative. I made friends. And most importantly, that's when I met Shivam—the love of my life.

Shivam, with his infectious enthusiasm, taught me to "dream big." While I saw myself as an average girl with average dreams, he wouldn't have any of it. He opened my eyes to my strengths – my communication skills, my marketing savvy, my talent for dance. He also encouraged me to work on my weaknesses, like physical fitness (not necessarily weight, but overall health and strength). I still remember him teaching me kickboxing and how to handle difficult situations if I ever found myself alone. His message was simple: dream big, anything is possible – all I had to do was believe in myself. He saw something unique in me, a potential I hadn't even recognized.

My friends played a huge role in my journey, too. They were my constant source of positivity—always there, cheering me on, always believing in me when I struggled to believe in myself. Our conversations were never about gossip or trivial things; they were about growth, dreams, and making our lives meaningful. Every time we talked, I felt lighter, inspired, and more confident about the person I was becoming. It was the kind of friendship that made you feel truly seen, truly valued, and inspired to push yourself to be your best self.

I remember those college days, sitting in my friend's cozy room while we were supposed to be studying. It was one of those afternoons when the air was filled with the sound of flipping pages, the soft hum of the fan above, and our voices mingling with laughter and hopes for the future. I said, with a bit of determination in my voice, "I really want to achieve something. I don't want to just sit at home and spend my husband's money."

She looked at me, her eyes sparkling with the same fire, and said, "Yeah, me too. I mean, I want to spend money... lots of it... but I want it to be my own."

I couldn't help but grin, "Exactly! Why should we have to ask someone else for money to spend, when we're more than capable of taking care of ourselves, even covering their expenses if we need to?" We both laughed, and for a moment, it felt like the world outside didn't exist—just two friends, full of dreams and possibilities.

She laughed, her voice light and carefree, "Yes, Pankhu, I just hope we don't turn into those aunties who are always gossiping about Sharma ji ki beti." We both burst into laughter, the sound of our shared joke ringing through the room, the tension from the day melting away.

And then I got serious for a moment. "But, you know, I don't just want to be a career-driven woman. I want to build a career and still have time to take care of my family and my future kids. I just want to be independent... and travel. Like, really travel."

She grinned, her face lighting up with the same excitement. "Ditto! But first, we'll have to pass this BBA!"

I groaned, pretending to be frustrated. "That's the only thing that's holding me back!" And once again, we both laughed, the innocence in our voices blending with the excitement of youthful dreams.

It was funny how simple those dreams felt back then. Life seemed so straightforward, like a path just waiting to be walked. But looking back, I realize how deeply those innocent aspirations shaped the way I see the world now. They were the seeds of independence, ambition, and the joy of dreaming big—without knowing just how much we were capable of achieving.

However, there was a period where I lost my way. I fell in with a different crowd, one that focused heavily on appearances – the latest trends, expensive clothes, and constant critiques- "fat bod," "big teeth," "less hair" – chipped away at my self-esteem. I stopped taking pictures, stopped enjoying the way I dressed. My focus shifted from talent to appearances.

Shivam, ever vigilant, intervened again. He gave me a much-needed wake-up call, reminding me of who I was and why I was changing. He helped me see that this wasn't me, that I was already beautiful as I am. He also realized it was time for me to change my social circle.

He unknowingly gifted me the key to my future career – an online psychology diploma course. Little did he know when he signed me up for that online psychology diploma course that it would become the foundation of my future career – a future he wouldn't be here to witness.

The Lesson

These experiences taught me a powerful lesson: the people you surround yourself with have a profound impact on your life. Seek out those who uplift you, who celebrate your strengths, and who challenge you to be your best self. Avoid those who bring you down or make you feel insecure. Choose your company wisely, because the people you spend time with can make or break your journey.

A Simple Exercise for Reflection

Keep a daily journal where you reflect on your interactions with others. Note how these interactions make you feel and whether they contribute to your personal growth or detract from it. Use this awareness to guide your future social choices.

Lesson 05

Religious Teachings Are Not Enough

The festive air of Ganesh Puja filled our society with excitement. The tradition of preparing a 56 Bhog—a grand offering of 56 dishes—was in full swing, with each family contributing a delicacy. The children were especially thrilled, their wide eyes and impatient fidgeting reflecting their eagerness to taste the treats after the aarti. Cheeku, my son, was no different.

"Mumma, I want everything on my plate, especially the chocolate laddus!" he exclaimed, practically bouncing in place as he eyed the offerings.

I smiled at his innocence and assured him we'd do our best. As the aarti concluded, a small stampede of children and adults made their way to the food. Plates piled high with delicacies were quickly handed out, and Cheeku and I managed to grab a fair share before the tables started to empty.

We found a spot to sit and began to eat, but a glance over my shoulder stopped me mid-bite. Near the food tables, I noticed the guard's children standing quietly with their mother. Their longing gazes fell on the diminishing platters, but they didn't move forward.

The mother held them back, her firm grip speaking a silent language: "Wait. This is not for us yet."

It pained me to watch. Their mother's restrained posture, the children's hesitant glances—it was a quiet reminder of the unspoken inequalities that exist even in moments meant to unite us.

Cheeku, oblivious to this, was busy savoring his food. But something stirred inside me, and I turned to him. "Cheeku," I said gently, "how about we share some of our prasad with those children?"

His brow furrowed. "But I want to eat this! It's mine," he protested, clutching his plate protectively.

I knelt beside him, keeping my voice calm. "Remember how upset you were when we almost missed the chocolate laddus? That's how they must be feeling right now. Let's share before it's too late."

After a moment of hesitation, he nodded reluctantly. Together, we approached the family. Cheeku, still a little unsure, offered the items he didn't particularly like. I noticed one of the children's eyes flicker toward the chocolate laddus on our plate, but he said nothing, his mother's quiet discipline keeping him in check.

I crouched down and held out the plate to him. "Would you like anything else?" I asked.

His face brightened, but before he could respond, his mother intervened. "No, no. This is enough. Thank you," she said firmly.

I pretended not to hear her. Instead, I smiled and gently asked the boy again. This time, he pointed shyly at the laddus.

"No! That's mine!" Cheeku shouted, pulling the plate closer.

The boy immediately withdrew his hand, but I turned to Cheeku. "Can you really eat all of them now?" I asked softly.

He didn't respond, but I could see him thinking. I reminded him again of his own disappointment earlier, how unfair it had felt. Slowly, his grip loosened, and with a reluctant sigh, he handed over one laddu.

"Just one," he said, his tone half-defiant, half-resigned.

As we walked back to our seat, I saw a spark of understanding in Cheeku's eyes. And as I reflected on the day later that night, I felt a bittersweet realization settle in: we teach our children to worship gods, to pray for their blessings, and to celebrate the divine. But often, we fail to teach them how to extend those blessings to others, how to truly embody the values we preach.

A few weeks later, during Paryushan Parv, a significant festival for Jains, we visited a Jain Tirth. The atmosphere was serene, the chants of prayers echoing in the air. I watched as a five-year-old boy stood beside his parents, reciting prayers with a confidence that belied his age. His parents beamed with pride, and I couldn't help but admire their dedication to teaching him the tenets of Jainism.

"That could be Cheeku someday," I thought, envisioning him performing rituals with the same sincerity.

After the prayers, we moved to the canteen area to rest. The same family from the temple was nearby, and the boy began to play while his parents chatted. At first, he threw a small stone at the canteen door. Then, he started tossing bits of garbage on the ground.

The canteen owner, a soft-spoken man, approached the boy politely. "Beta, please don't do that. It's not good for the temple premises."

The boy ignored him, and his parents, though clearly aware, chose not to intervene.

The mischief escalated. The boy began throwing garbage at the canteen door, and this time, the owner hesitated before addressing the parents directly.

"Sir, ma'am, could you please ask your child to stop? This is a holy place, and it's important to keep it clean," he requested humbly.

The parents looked up briefly. "Can't you let him play for a while? We're leaving in ten minutes," the father replied dismissively.

The owner nodded and walked away, visibly disheartened. I sat there, watching the scene unfold, and a wave of realization washed over me.

We often take immense pride in instilling religious values in our children, teaching them prayers, rituals, and the importance of faith. Yet, we overlook the basic human values that form the foundation of those teachings—respect for others, concern for the environment, and love for all living beings.

That day, I resolved to teach Cheeku not just the rituals of religion but also the essence of humanity. Religious practices may connect us to the divine, but it's our actions—our respect, empathy, and kindness—that truly reflect the teachings of the gods we worship.

The Lesson

Religious teachings are essential, but they are not enough. Without core human values, rituals lose their meaning. As parents, it's our responsibility to guide the next generation toward not just worshipping the divine but also embodying it in their actions.

A Simple Exercise for Reflection

Brainstorm: Spend 5 minutes free-writing a list of values that are important to you.

Some examples: honesty, compassion, integrity, justice, kindness, courage, freedom, equality, creativity, perseverance, respect, responsibility.

Prioritize:

1. **Narrow it down:** Choose the 5-7 values that are MOST important to you.
    - **Rank them:** Order these values from most important to least important.
    - **Consider:** How do these values guide your decisions and actions in daily life?
2. **Reflect:**
    - **Identify inconsistencies:** Are there any situations where your actions don't align with your stated values?
    - **Set intentions:** How can you better live in accordance with your core values?
3. **Create reminders:** Find ways to keep your values top-of-mind (e.g., write them down

Lesson 06

The Value of People Over Possessions

When I think back to my teenage years, I see a version of myself that clung fiercely to her belongings, as though they were extensions of her soul. My earrings, dresses, books, and even something as trivial as a decorative pen—all of it mattered deeply. I didn't grow up in extravagance; getting something new wasn't a given. Every item I owned felt earned, a victory I didn't take lightly. I wore my possessiveness as a badge of honor, unapologetically.

One summer during my school days, I remember my cousin borrowing a pair of my favorite earrings. They were delicate, silver hoops with tiny charms—one of the few pieces of jewelry I had saved up for. When she returned them, one of the charms was missing, and the clasp was bent. "How could you not take care of them?" I had cried. The idea of someone mishandling something I valued so much felt almost like a betrayal. She apologized, but I sulked for days. My cousin avoided borrowing anything from me after that, and though I was relieved at the time, I now wonder if I valued those earrings more than her companionship.

The High-Heeled Incident

Fast forward to my adulthood, and that same possessiveness lingered. One incident, in particular, stands out. My younger sister, Manya, was visiting me in Indore. She had always been the free-spirited one, a stark contrast to my cautious, meticulous nature. One morning, she found her way to my shoe rack, her eyes lighting up at the sight of my favorite pair of high heels.

Now, these weren't just any heels. They were a glossy nude pair that I had saved up for months to buy. Every time I wore them, they made me feel confident and elegant, as though they carried a piece of my hard-earned pride. So, when Manya decided to try them on without asking me.

What happened next was predictable yet infuriating. As she attempted to walk in them, her foot twisted, and she tumbled to the floor. The sound of snapping heels jolted me out of my sleep. Rushing to the living room, I saw her sprawled on the floor, my precious heels broken beyond repair.

"Do you even realize what you've done?" I yelled, snatching the shoes from her hands. "Why would you touch my things without asking?"

Manya looked at me, stunned and slightly embarrassed. "I just wanted to try them on. I didn't mean to break them," she said softly, rubbing her ankle.

My parents and aunt rushed in, trying to diffuse the tension. "It's just a pair of shoes," my mom reasoned. "You can always get another one."

But I wasn't ready to listen. "You don't understand!" I cried. "These shoes aren't just shoes. They represent my hard work!"

Looking back, I cringe at how I handled that situation. My sister, who adored me, had been hurt, and all I could think about was my shoes. The memory still stings, not because of the broken heels, but because of the opportunity I lost to show love and understanding.

Life has a way of putting things into perspective, often through the most painful experiences. Losing Shivam, my husband and my partner in every sense, shattered me. In the wake of his passing, the things I had once fiercely guarded seemed laughably insignificant.

I realized now that these materialistic possessions—none of them are mine! They can be taken away just like that, in a blink. But our relationships, the bonds we nurture with people, don't fade away as easily.

In those first few weeks, friends and relatives came to visit, offering their condolences and often rummaging through my wardrobe without asking. My sarees were handled carelessly, some never put back properly. Had this happened before, I would have been livid. But now, I didn't care. My focus was elsewhere—on the gaping void in my life that no possession could ever fill.

Packing up our shared home after Shivam's passing was one of the most heart-wrenching experiences of my life. My in-laws, thinking practically, decided that much of our furniture and belongings should be taken away. "Where will you keep all this?" they asked, believing they were doing me a favor. And so, our life together—the crockery we'd picked out, the books we'd read side by side, the décor we'd chosen—was packed up and sent away.

All I was left with was our bedroom furniture and a few of Shivam's clothes. Among them was a simple, worn T-shirt that he used to wear on lazy Sunday mornings. Finding it one day as I unpacked, I held it to my chest, inhaling the faint trace of his scent that still lingered. Tears streamed down my face. "This is all I have left of him," I thought. But then I realized something: Shivam wasn't in that T-shirt or in any of the items that had been taken away. He was in the memories, the love, and the lessons he left behind. He was in the laughter we shared on lazy Sunday mornings, in the way he hummed his favorite songs while cooking, and in the quiet strength he gave me when I doubted myself. He was in the way our son instinctively sought something to rub his fingers against, like an elbow, while deep in thought—just as Shivam used to fidget with the edge of a fabric with pico stitching, finding comfort in its texture. Every corner of my life was infused with pieces of him, far beyond the tangible items we had collected together.

It hit me then: while possessions could be lost, damaged, or taken away, the essence of someone—their love, their values, their impact on your life—remains eternal. Shivam's presence wasn't confined to a T-shirt or a set of crockery; it lived in the way he had shaped me into the person I was.

That realization began to shift something deep within me. It wasn't an immediate change—I still felt the sting of loss and the temptation to cling to what little I had left. But over time, I started to let go of my attachment to things and focus instead on preserving and cherishing the intangible legacy he had left behind.

Infact one day, as I watched my son play with his toys, I realized that he didn't care about how expensive or perfect they were. What mattered to him was the time I spent with him, the stories I told, and the games we played together. This innocence, this ability to value people over possessions, was something I vowed to nurture in myself.

Today, I try to focus less on material things and more on creating meaningful connections. When Manya visits now, I let her raid my wardrobe, shoes and all. If she spills coffee on a saree, it's just a saree. What matters is the laughter we share, the bond we've rebuilt after years of my possessiveness.

The Lesson

Possessions can bring temporary happiness, but they're no substitute for the love and connection we share with others. Losing Shivam taught me that life's true treasures aren't things we can hold in our hands but the people we hold in our hearts. Today, I strive to cherish those around me, knowing that they are the real source of joy and meaning. Everything else? It's just stuff.

A Simple Exercise for Reflection

If you're someone who values possessions deeply, here's an exercise to help shift your perspective:

- Create a Memory Inventory: List three items you consider valuable. For each, write down the memories or people associated with it. Reflect on whether it's the item or the connection that holds true value.
- Practice Generosity: Give away something you hold dear to someone who needs it more. Notice how it feels to prioritize their happiness over your attachment.

Lesson 07

Knocking Twice: A Lesson in Respect

Back in 2013-2014, I was known for being overly trusting. When someone told me we had to meet at a specific time and place, I treated it like a signed agreement, believing their word was final and unchangeable. I would plan my entire day accordingly, making sure to arrive on time. This was a bad habit, planning everything in advance and organizing my day to avoid redundant travel. Shivam, on the other hand, was my complete opposite. He never took plans seriously, changing them as situations arose. He could never give a straight answer about his day's plans. You can imagine the friction between us when these two opposite personalities came together.

One fine day, after we had become a couple and were comfortable advising and pointing out each other's mistakes, I had a meeting with a potential client during my mutual fund internship. The meeting was scheduled 30 minutes before my usual office hours, meaning I had to leave home at 8 am, an hour earlier than usual. It was June in Indore, known for unexpected rains. Shivam often drove alongside me on a separate bike to ensure I reached my office without getting stuck in the rain.

The day before the meeting, I panicked and told him he didn't need to come the next morning, but if he wanted to drop me, he had to be on time at 7:45 am (knowing he might not take it seriously). The night before, he told me, "Arey baba, I will come no matter what. But first, at least text the client and confirm tomorrow's meeting." Annoyed, I replied, "Why confirm? When he said it once, it means it's final. We are all grown-ups, mature enough to keep our word. Who needs constant reminders?"

He insisted, "You never know if he forgot or if something came up. Just ask or at least tell him you'll be seeing him tomorrow." Stubbornly, I said, "No! I'm not going to disturb him. I'll just be there on time."

The next morning, Shivam came as promised, and I reached the client's office only to find it closed. Dreading the inevitable lecture, I avoided eye contact and called the client. He admitted he had forgotten about the meeting. Shivam had a whole lecture ready for me. Despite my annoyance, I had to admit he was right this time.

Listening to his endless rant on how I never listen to him and how correct he was, I silently endured until he dropped me at my office. My irritation grew as he continued, pausing only when I glared at him. Our usual Tom and Jerry dynamic was in full swing, but little did I know it was shaping me into who I am today.

Despite this lesson, I didn't learn immediately. Another time, we had a casual dinner plan with one of Shivam's friends. I pre-planned everything again. This time, we didn't want to have dinner, and Shivam gave them indirect cues about our busy schedules and upcoming exams, hoping they'd take the hint. But this friend insisted on coming over, staying at Shivam's place, and having dinner with us, much to Shivam's frustration.

Shivam explained, "Some people don't understand basic etiquette. They don't get the cues that the other party isn't interested or that the timing isn't right. Due to our humbleness, we can't say no directly, and some people take advantage of that. In the long run, these relationships don't survive because they don't respect the other person's boundaries, privacy, or willingness to host them."

I asked him to adjust a bit since they were his friends and genuinely wanted to meet. But he was certain they just wanted a free place to stay while exploring Indore.

As it turned out, Shivam was right again. They just wanted a place to stay and explore Indore. I had planned my day around the dinner, but 30 minutes before the scheduled time, we found out they weren't coming. I was slightly disappointed but also braced for Shivam's "I told you so" lecture.

Shivam was relieved, as we ended up having a personal dinner, but I had a new understanding. People are not always as reliable as they seem. Sometimes, their intentions are genuine, and sometimes they are not. Since then, I started to not just double-check but triple-check before confirming meetings. I also learned to keep my plans flexible, allowing for last-minute changes.

The Lesson

This experience taught me the importance of respecting other people's time and boundaries. It also emphasized the need to balance trust with caution. I've learned to value my own time and not overextend myself for others who may not reciprocate the same level of commitment. Now, I ensure my plans are fluid, understanding that sometimes things don't go as expected. And most importantly, I've learned to maintain my self-esteem and self-worth, understanding that true respect comes from both sides.

I also realized that genuine invitations shouldn't be taken for granted. Today, I only stay with people when I feel 100% welcome. Otherwise, I understand that everyone has busy, hectic lives, and staying at a hotel is perfectly fine. If you truly want to spend time with someone, it's better to mutually agree on a time and place where both parties can enjoy the time together.

A Simple Exercise for Reflection

Think about a recent situation where a plan didn't go as expected. How did you react? Were you rigid, like the "old me," expecting everything to go as agreed, or were you more flexible, like Shivam, adjusting to the changes?

1. Write down a plan that didn't go as you imagined (a canceled meeting, a late friend, a change of schedule).

2. Reflect on how you reacted. Did you feel frustrated or disappointed? Or were you able to adapt calmly?

3. Practice flexibility: For your next plan, prepare for the possibility that things might change. How will you manage your emotions if they do? Write down two ways you can adapt the next time plans fall through.

Bonus: Try not to over-plan your day tomorrow. Let go of one commitment that isn't urgent and see how it feels!

Lesson 08

Breaking Free

Lately, I have been facing health issues again and again, despite living a healthy lifestyle. The doctors said it was due to stress, anxiety, and a lack of support. Their advice was clear—I needed a break from my surroundings. I tried taking one during family vacations, but nothing changed. The heaviness within me remained.

Hoping for a deeper understanding, I turned to therapy and healing sessions. Strangely, every therapist or healer I met pointed to the same question: *What if you didn't have anyone around you telling you how you should be? How do you see yourself?*

The realization hit me hard. Somewhere, at my core, my deepest value was freedom. And what I was truly craving was freedom from expectations—the pressure to fit into roles, to wear the clothes people wanted me to, to live a life shaped by others' definitions.

One of them suggested a solo trip. It sounded impossible. How could I leave without Cheeku? And my family—especially my mom—would never allow it. But just as I was debating this within myself, my health took a turn for the worse. Excessive burping, chest pains—it felt like my body was screaming for attention. The fear of a heart condition led me to acupuncture, where I was told my symptoms were due to *liver stagnation*—a condition caused by suppressed emotions.

That was my wake-up call. This time, I had to save myself. Without overthinking, I booked tickets to Goa—with my cousin. It wasn't entirely a solo trip, but for both of us, it was our first attempt at true independence.

Goa changed me in ways I still struggle to put into words. In just three days, something inside me shifted. I found myself smiling effortlessly. Confidence, which had felt lost for so long, slowly started returning. And the most surprising part? I didn't take a single medicine. My body, which had been suffocating under stress, was suddenly breathing freely—without force, without effort.

When I returned home, my mom, in her usual way, simplified everything: *You felt good there because you were able to wear what you wanted and live as you wanted.*

Maybe she was right. Maybe, for the first time in a long time, I was just *me*.

That's when I started reflecting on a truth that had been haunting me for years—*the burden of expectations.*

I've spent my life trapped in an endless tug-of-war between what I expect from the world and what it actually gives me. No matter how much I try to shed these expectations, they keep creeping back, dictating my thoughts, my actions, my sense of self.

Being a daughter, a sister, a wife, a mother, and a friend means carrying responsibilities. But somewhere along the way, I lost sight of who I was beneath those roles. As a daughter, I was expected to be obedient, even when my beliefs clashed with my family's. As a sister, I was supposed to be supportive, even when my own emotional reserves were empty. As a wife, I was meant to be patient and nurturing, even when my needs were ignored. And even now, I still hear people mentioning the arguments Shivam and I had—as if disagreements between husbands and wives aren't normal. As a mother, I'm expected to be perfect, to never falter, to always prioritize my child over myself.

Expectations don't just come from others; we impose them on ourselves too. I spent years trying to be the *perfect* version of everything—only to realize that perfection is an illusion. We beat ourselves up for not being ideal daughters, wives, mothers, or professionals, setting impossibly high standards that leave us feeling like failures. But life isn't about perfection. It's about *progress.* It's about embracing our flaws, making mistakes, and learning from them.

My trip to Goa made me realize something important: I don't have to meet every expectation. I don't have to be everything for everyone. And most importantly, I don't have to live by the standards others set for me—or even the unrealistic ones I set for myself.

Now, I am doing something different. I no longer expect people to always be there for me just because I need them or because their role in my life dictates they should be. Even my family—my in-laws, my brother, my parents, my uncles, aunts, and cousins—tell me not to worry about the future. They assure me, *We are here for you.* They say I don't need to worry about finances because they will stand by me.

But here's the truth: I once had many expectations from life—especially the one I had envisioned with Shivam. A future where we grew old together. A partnership built on dreams we were yet to fulfill. And in a single moment, all of those expectations shattered. There is no more Shivam. There is no life with him. And I am no longer the person I used to be.

So while I know my family is there for me, I can no longer fully trust life and what it has in store. Will it bring me joy, or will it bring more heartbreak?

I refuse to be vulnerable and dependent again. Instead of relying too much on others, I am learning to stand on my own. I am working towards becoming more capable, more self-reliant. Life will throw its challenges my way—sometimes blessings, sometimes storms—but I need to be prepared for all of it.

Expectations have always been a source of hurt for me, but I also understand that they are inescapable. No relationship, no endeavor can exist without them. Friendships thrive on the expectation of companionship. Marriages are built on the expectation of support. Even in careers, we expect effort to be rewarded.

But the key is balance. When we expect too much, we set ourselves up for disappointment. That's what I'm learning now—to expect, but not attach my happiness to those expectations. When disappointment comes, I acknowledge it and move forward. I no longer place the same weight on people or circumstances. I am learning to navigate life without holding on too tightly to outcomes.

I've also started setting boundaries. I tell people not to expect too much from me. I am working toward my goals, but I don't yet know where this journey will take me. I cannot promise that I will fulfill every expectation placed upon me—and that's okay.

Shivam himself taught me an invaluable lesson during his final days. One evening, while watching a movie, he turned to me and said:

"Pankhu, our baby will be our whole world. But promise me, in raising him, don't lose yourself. Don't expect too much from him just because we sacrificed for him. We will do what we do out of love, because we are parents. If he chooses to be there for us in our old age, we'll be lucky. But if not, don't hold him back. Don't expect too much."

That moment stayed with me. He saw life for what it truly is—unpredictable, uncontrollable. And now, I am learning to see it the same way. I'm trying to let go of the need to control, to release expectations, and to embrace whatever comes my way.

The Lesson

The truth lies somewhere in between—not in eliminating expectations entirely, but in managing them. It's about acknowledging that expectations are human, but not letting them dictate our happiness. It's about holding ourselves accountable without carrying the weight of the world's demands.

There's a fine line between expecting and being consumed by expectations. If we don't expect anything, we lose motivation. But if we expect too much, we set ourselves up for pain. The real trick is to find that midpoint—to hope, but not demand; to strive, but not suffer in the process.

Life doesn't come with guarantees, and I no longer expect it to. What I do know is this—I am capable. I am strong. And no matter what comes my way, I will walk this path on my own terms.

A Simple Exercise for Reflection

Expectations are inevitable, but they don't have to control your life. Take a moment to reflect on the expectations you have of yourself and others.

Identify Expectations:

- Write down a list of expectations you have for yourself. Do you expect perfection? Do you demand too much from yourself in certain areas?
- Now write down the expectations others seem to have of you. Are you constantly trying to live up to someone else's ideal?

Evaluate the Impact:

- Reflect on how these expectations affect your mental and emotional well-being. Do they motivate you or overwhelm you?
- Think about which expectations are healthy and which ones might be unrealistic or harmful.

Find the Midpoint:

- For each unrealistic expectation, find a middle ground. How can you adjust your expectations so they push you without overwhelming you?
- Consider what it would feel like to let go of certain expectations. Write down a few ways you can release those that no longer serve you.

Set New Intentions:

- Rather than focusing on expectations, set intentions. What kind of person do you want to be? How can you align your actions with that goal without placing unrealistic demands on yourself?

Lesson 09

Prioritize – Navigating the Shifting Tides of Life

What does it mean to prioritize? For most, it's about putting what's important first. But defining what's "important" isn't as simple as it seems. Priorities aren't static—they're deeply personal and often shaped by the circumstances we find ourselves in. This is something I learned through a series of decisions that tested my resolve, challenged societal expectations, and ultimately reshaped the way I look at life.

I still remember the day our principal walked into my eleventh-grade classroom. She was an elegant South Indian woman, always impeccably dressed in a saree, her face adorned with a calm yet commanding expression. Her mere presence brought the noisy class to a standstill.

As she began to speak, her tone was gentle yet firm, carrying the weight of her words. She asked each of us a simple question:

"What matters most to you right now? How do you spend your time?"

One by one, my classmates gave their answers:

"Spending time with family."

"Exercising regularly."

"Attending singing classes."

Most of us assumed this was just another motivational talk about focusing on academics. But what she said next caught us by surprise:

"Your answers are valid because everyone has different priorities. What matters most to one person might not matter at all to another. But here's the thing—your priorities should align with the stage of life you're in. For you, eleventh and twelfth grade are pivotal years. Right now, your education should take precedence, because the decisions you make today will shape your future."

Her words hit me hard. I realized I didn't have a clear sense of what my priorities were. I was the eldest daughter in a middle-class family, and while my parents supported me in every way they could, they never pressured me to chase grades or pursue specific career paths. They valued true learning and life experiences over societal benchmarks.

At first, I felt lucky to have such freedom. But as I sat there listening to my principal, I began to wonder: Was this freedom a gift or a challenge? I didn't know what path to follow, and without guidance, I felt adrift.

Years later, when I completed my 12th grade, I knew I wanted to study psychology. The field fascinated me, and I could see myself building a career in it. But life, as it often does, had other plans.

There weren't many good psychology programs in my state, and the thought of sending me to Delhi or Bangalore for studies was too much for my father. He worried about my health and my age, and he just wasn't ready to let me go so far from home. Instead, he suggested I pursue biology and become a doctor.

I refused, but by the time the debates and discussions ended, I had missed the application deadlines for most psychology programs. My only viable option was a Bachelor's in Business Administration (BBA)—a field I had never even considered. Reluctantly, I enrolled, putting aside my dreams for the sake of practicality.

Two years later, as my BBA program neared its end, the idea of studying psychology resurfaced. Shivam, my then-boyfriend, was incredibly supportive. He suggested we pursue our post-graduate studies together in the same city, even if our fields were different. His support gave me hope, and for a brief moment, it felt like my dream was within reach.

But once again, family concerns came into play. My father wasn't comfortable with the idea of me leaving home, and I found myself prioritizing his wishes over my aspirations. I chose to stay in Indore and pursue a Master's in Business Administration (MBA).

This decision, made out of love and duty, left me feeling detached. I attended classes but lacked the passion or drive to excel. The idea of psychology began to feel like a distant memory, something I had wanted but could no longer have.

After completing my MBA, my focus shifted to marriage. Shivam and I had decided to build a life together, and my priorities aligned with that vision. Long-term jobs and further studies abroad didn't fit into the plans we had for our future family.

I took up a short-term teaching position as a visiting faculty, which was fulfilling in some ways but far from financially rewarding. My sense of purpose felt lost, and I began to question whether I had sacrificed too much.

One evening, during a candid conversation, Shivam asked me to consider pursuing psychology again, even suggesting that I study abroad on my own. While his encouragement was sincere, it also highlighted a stark difference in our priorities.

I asked him, "What are your top three priorities?"

Without hesitation, he replied, "Family, career, and friends."

At first, his answer annoyed me. I felt unseen and unacknowledged, as though I wasn't a significant part of his life. I pushed back, saying, "Your priorities aren't what you think they are. They're your family, friends, and then me."

But Shivam, ever thoughtful, clarified with a smile, "When I say family, that includes you too. You're the most important part of it."

His reassurance calmed me momentarily, but it also forced me to reflect. Was I being unfair to him by expecting our priorities to mirror each other's? Was I letting my own sacrifices cloud my understanding of his intentions? He then asked, "What are your top priorities?" I answered sarcastically, "Unlike you, my first priority is you and us, then my family and career." He corrected me gently, "This is where you're wrong, Pankhu. Why are you putting your career last? Your career is part of you, and you should prioritize yourself first." It's funny, isn't it? He was teaching me to love myself and put myself first, even though his own list didn't reflect the same thing!

He continued, "I can't appreciate enough how you've tried to adapt to my family and our culture. But, Pankhu, I don't want you to lose yourself in all this." I replied, "But it's too late now. I won't leave without you, and you won't be able to leave India." He then said, "Pankhu, it's my dream that you become a psychologist." I scoffed, "I don't see that happening anytime soon." He countered, "It's my priority now. Once the baby arrives, you won't have to worry about earning. I'll take care of everything. I'll hire a nanny, and you will study psychology. Your first priority should be you. Just understand, when you love yourself, you make me happy." I decided to rearrange my own priorities, but as you know, life had other plans. He wasn't there after the baby's arrival to take care of everything. How could I stick to that priority list? Just three months later, I was desperately searching for any source of income – teaching, dance choreography, tarot, graphology, tuition… anything. But somewhere, his words echoed in my mind: "When you love yourself, you make me happy." And I always want him to be happy, wherever he is. So, I enrolled in a distance psychology course. Studying again with the trauma, the responsibilities, and the memory issues… it wasn't easy. But maybe, not for the love of myself, but for him, I put my career on that list, still at number three. And today, here I am, a psychologist, living my dream… or rather, his dream.

It was in that moment I realized: Priorities don't have to look the same to align. His family included me, even if he didn't always say it explicitly. And while I felt undervalued at times, it was my responsibility to communicate my needs, just as he had communicated his.

Looking back, I see how my priorities shifted at every stage of life. Sometimes, those shifts were deliberate; other times, they were dictated by circumstances. But the one constant was the need to reevaluate and adapt.

The principal's lesson still rings true: Prioritizing is not just about making a list—it's about understanding what truly matters at a given time and aligning your actions with those values.

The Lesson

Love and duty can intertwine with personal aspirations: My choices were often driven by love for my family and a sense of duty, but those choices also shaped my path and, eventually, led me back to my own aspirations.

Priorities are fluid, especially in the face of loss: What I prioritized before Shivam's passing drastically changed afterward. Grief, motherhood, and the need to survive reshaped my focus, forcing me to redefine what truly mattered.

Self-love can be a driving force, even when it's not immediately apparent: Shivam's words about self-prioritization stayed with me, even after he was gone. Though it took time and difficult circumstances, those words ultimately spurred me to pursue my dream, not just for him, but for myself.

Dreams can be realized, even after detours and delays: My path to becoming a psychologist was far from straightforward, but it shows that dreams can still come true, even after significant detours and delays. It's a testament to resilience and the power of never fully letting go of what you're passionate about.

Life is a series of crossroads, each requiring a choice. Choose what matters most to you, and trust that those decisions will lead you to where you're meant to be.

A Simple Exercise for Reflection

Think about it:

What are the most important things in your life right now? How do you prioritize your time and energy between different aspects of your life?

Have your priorities changed over time? What factors have influenced these changes?

Lesson 10

The Tightrope Walk: Balancing Relationships, Boundaries, and Self-Worth

Growing up, my mom, a woman I call "Mahaan Atma" (great soul), instilled in us the belief that it is always better to take a step back and apologize to maintain peace and longevity in relationships. Sometimes, I find her views conservative. She believes that if one wants to have lasting relationships and family bonds, they must practice adjusting and saying sorry, as it is better than creating distance or breaking the bond. On the other hand, I often wondered what is the use of such people or the need for such family if every time we have to pay the price of our self-esteem just to keep them in our lives. As social animals, we need connections to rely on, support us, and understand us. But if all this is expected from only one or two people in the family or friendship, it raises the question of whether they really are your friends and family or not.

Despite my disagreements with her, I found myself clinging to my mom's advice, especially in friendships. One such friend was Lilly, a blunt and honest girl I met in school. We were close, but her short temper clashed with my laid-back personality. Often, missed appointments on my part sparked her anger, and I'd resort to elaborate apologies – a strategy I borrowed from boyfriend behavior, complete with chocolates and multiple "sorrys."

This dynamic reached a turning point in 2012-2013, during my graduation years. We planned to meet at her place one evening, but I ran late, possibly because I was with Shivam. Anticipating the usual routine, I braced myself for the appeasement dance.

Arriving at her house, I found her fuming silently. Apologies tumbled out of me, but they were met with stony silence. After several failed attempts, she finally said, "Leave." Initially shocked, I naively tried again, promising it wouldn't happen again. Her even harsher response, "Pankh, just LEAVE," finally registered. And this time, I did.

Leaving her house that day, a wave of hurt washed over me, mingled with a newfound resolve. I promised myself: no more automatic apologies unless I was truly in the wrong. More importantly, I wouldn't chase after someone who didn't respect my time or boundaries.

Since then, Lilly and I have reconnected and drifted apart a few times. She even met Shivam and was genuinely happy for me. While I know her heart is good, some words leave lasting scars. Healthy relationships, whether friendships or romantic ones, thrive on mutual respect and effort. Everyone deserves to feel valued, and sometimes, letting go of those who don't reciprocate that feeling is necessary.

This experience taught me a valuable lesson: constant apologies and one-sided efforts can erode self-respect. While maintaining relationships is important, it shouldn't come at the expense of our dignity. Over time, I've learned to navigate this tightrope walk – balancing peace with self-worth. True connections are built on a foundation of mutual understanding and respect. And sometimes, walking away from those who don't contribute to that foundation is the best way to preserve your own well-being. These lessons have shaped me into a more self-aware individual, understanding that while peace is important, it should never come at the cost of sacrificing my self-respect.

Around the same time, I had another realization—one that Shivam, unknowingly, helped me understand.

Growing up, I truly believed that love and meaningful relationships were defined by how much time and energy you were willing to give others. I lived by this principle. I thought that being available, no matter what, was the ultimate expression of care and loyalty. It wasn't something I expected from others—I wanted to embody it myself.

But over time, I learned that constantly being there for others, without setting boundaries, can lead to exhaustion and feelings of being undervalued. The lesson didn't come easily—it was one that life taught me in subtle, and sometimes painful, ways.

It was 2014, and I was in the middle of my graduation years. My life revolved around a small but close-knit circle of friends. They were everything to me. If someone needed me for anything—whether it was shopping, studying, or simply sharing stories—I was always the first to show up.

Being single and free of many responsibilities, I filled my time with my friends, prioritizing their needs and happiness over my own. I thought this was what friendship meant: to always be present, always ready to help. But I never stopped to ask myself if this constant availability was affecting how I valued myself—or how others valued me.

One day, I had an emotional fallout with a close friend. I was hurt, upset, and couldn't focus on my studies, even though our exams were just two days away. I called Mishka, one of my closest friends at the time. Mishka was someone I trusted deeply—she had a kind heart and a calming presence.

When I told her I wasn't in the right frame of mind to study, she listened empathetically and said, "Come over at 1 pm after my coaching class. We'll study together, and it'll help you concentrate." Her words reassured me. It felt good to know I had someone to lean on.

At sharp 1 pm, I reached her house, eager to find some comfort. Her mother opened the door and greeted me warmly but with a hint of surprise. "Hello Pankhuri! How are you? Does Mishka know you're coming?"

Her question made me hesitate. "Yes, aunty," I replied, trying to sound confident. "She asked me to come at 1."

Her mother smiled politely and said, "Why don't you call her and check where she is?"

I pulled out my phone and called Mishka, but she didn't pick up. After a few attempts, I received a text: Running a bit late. Meet me at 2 instead.

It wasn't malicious, just casual—perhaps too casual for the state I was in. She probably didn't realize how much I was counting on her presence that day. But standing there, feeling out of place and unwanted, my heart sank. I muttered an excuse to her mother and left, unsure of how to spend the next hour.

I had no idea where to go. I wandered aimlessly until I decided to visit a classmate's PG. This classmate, someone I barely spoke to outside of exchanging notes, welcomed me warmly. She asked if I could help her with a topic she was struggling with. I nodded, trying to focus, but the hurt inside me bubbled up.

As she started asking questions, I couldn't hold back my tears. When she asked what was wrong, I lied, saying I was overwhelmed with exam stress. Deep down, I didn't want to admit the truth—that I felt rejected and insignificant to someone I considered a close friend.

At 2 pm, I finally met Mishka outside her coaching center. She apologized for running late and, as always, greeted me with her easygoing charm. She introduced me to her friends, including Shivam—a classmate of mine I had never spoken to directly.

Mishka didn't mean to hurt me earlier, but her casual approach to our plans highlighted something important: I had made her a priority in my life, but she didn't see me the same way. It wasn't intentional on her part—she simply didn't realize the depth of my emotions.

That day, Mishka and her friends invited me to join their group for a birthday celebration, followed by a group study session. I reluctantly agreed. My heart still felt heavy, but I decided to push through and join them.

During the group study, I found myself sitting next to Shivam. We were solving a math problem together when he suddenly paused and scribbled something on a piece of paper. He wrote the number 2 several times, interspersed with a single number 6. Sliding the paper toward me, he asked, "What do you see?"

I replied, "There's a 6 among all these 2s."

He smiled and said, "Exactly. The 6 stands out because it's rare. When something is always available, like the 2s, people stop noticing it. But the moment something becomes less available, it becomes more valuable.

"The same happens in life," he continued. "If you're always there—always ready, always giving—people start to take you for granted. It's not because they don't care about you; it's because they don't realize how much you're giving. That's why it's important to create balance. Be there for people, but don't be too available. Let there be a sense of freshness in your presence."

Shivam's words stayed with me. For years, I had conditioned myself to believe that being constantly available was a virtue, but now I saw how it had affected my relationships. My friends didn't mean to take me for granted—they had simply become accustomed to my presence, just as I had trained them to.

From that day on, I began setting boundaries. I stopped saying yes to everything and started prioritizing my own needs. It wasn't easy. At first, some people thought I was being distant or aloof. But I wasn't being unkind—I was learning to respect myself.

The Lesson

Through my journey, I've learned that **balance is everything**.

- If you **give too much**, you lose yourself.
- If you **give too little**, you lose connection.
- True relationships thrive when there is **mutual effort, respect, and understanding**.

As my mom always said, **adjustment is necessary—but never at the cost of your self-respect.**

Shivam taught me a profound truth: **relationships thrive on balance. Being there for others is important, but so is being there for yourself. Constant availability can lead to being taken for granted—not because people don't care, but because they don't see the effort you're putting in.**

Today, I value my time and energy. I still enjoy being there for the people I care about, but I do so in a way that respects my boundaries. If my efforts aren't reciprocated equally, I step back.

This doesn't make me selfish; it makes me self-aware. And in valuing myself, I've learned to create healthier, more meaningful connections.

A Simple Exercise for Reflection

The Relationship Balance Sheet

Step 1: Create two columns:

- **Strengthens You** – List people who respect your boundaries and uplift you.
- **Weakens You** – List those who drain you, disrespect your time, or don't reciprocate effort.

Step 2: Reflection

- Are you investing **more time** in people who strengthen or weaken you?
- Have you been **apologizing too much** or **compromising your self-worth**?

Step 3: Action Plan

- **Set Boundaries** – Choose one small boundary to implement today.
- **Nurture Positive Bonds** – Strengthen relationships that uplift you.
- **Let Go** – Distance yourself from draining relationships.

Bonus Challenge: Track how often you **over-apologize** this week. Ask yourself: *Was it really necessary?*

Lesson 11

No Learning is Ever Wasted

This lesson is a big part of my personality. Ever since childhood, I've had a deep curiosity to keep learning and growing, whether it was something I excelled at, like dance, or something entirely new. For me, learning wasn't just about mastering a skill—it was about satisfying my curiosity and understanding how things work. From facials, waxing, baking, cooking, dancing, candle making, bouquet making, tie-dye, jewelry making, table tennis (reluctantly), grooming classes—the list goes on, and that was just during my childhood.

Friends and relatives often asked, "Why learn all this? How will it help your career?" At first, I used to reply naively, saying things like, "Maybe one day I'll open a salon or design jewelry." My ambitions shifted frequently, and I even enrolled in a fashion design course for a while. However, after finishing my master's degree and still lacking a stable career, I began to question my choices. I regretted spending time on unusual skills while my classmates remained focused and goal-oriented. I sometimes avoided confronting this inner conflict by making excuses for myself and others, blaming circumstances or my lack of clarity. Sometimes, I even blamed my parents for forcing me into academic streams I didn't want to pursue. I'd say, "I am stuck because I did what you wanted, not what I wanted!". My father, in response, always told me:

"No learning is ever wasted. It will serve you in ways you cannot see yet."

And my mother would add, "Beta, career skills are important, but learning different things will help you face life's challenges."

At that time, I didn't really understand their words. It wasn't until the COVID-19 pandemic that these lessons started making sense.

Just six months into my marriage with Shivam, the pandemic hit, turning everyone's world upside down. I was already adjusting to life in his hometown, where there weren't many modern salons or shops. Thanks to the grooming skills I learned in 11th grade, I was able to take care of myself. I used my cooking skills to fit into my new role as a daughter-in-law. Meanwhile, I was also preparing for the UGC-NET exam, which was scheduled for December. But life had other plans.

In November, my mom's health suddenly worsened, showing signs of a second heart attack. Like many mothers, she tried to carry on without worrying the family. I was anxious, distracted from my studies, torn between my duties and concern for her. Exhausted from house chores, I struggled to study, and when I finally gave the exam, I knew it wasn't my best. Two days later, I got a call—Mom was in the hospital. I couldn't hold back the tears—all I wanted was to be in Indore with her. Shivam searched for travel options, but trains were booked, and flights were unavailable. My mother-in-law urged us to wait for tickets, but I couldn't wait any longer. After connecting through multiple buses, we finally reached Indore by night.

Seeing my mom in that condition, I felt like I could lose her at any moment. I was also angry that she never took a break from work to rest. But, as always, she simply said, "My work is my life. I'd die without it." We were all speechless.

Three to four days later, Shivam returned home, and his parents and elder brother came to visit my mom and take me back. During this visit, our pre-decided plans of settling in Indore after a year were discussed between the families. After some conversations, the decision was made that I would return to Indore alone if I found a job, as Shivam's family wasn't ready to send him due to some astrological predictions. I wasn't keen on coming back to Indore alone, but Shivam assured me that he'd join me in a few months.

I got a job as a visiting faculty member at my previous college and another one. We also decided to expand my mom's boutique by starting a women's wedding apparel line, which would help her as well.

For two months, I juggled two jobs and managed all the preparations for the business—material procurement, designing, and stitching—while darting back and forth between the colleges, my mom's boutique, and the market. During my drives and breaks, I frequently spoke on Bluetooth with my mother-in-law and Shivam, both of whom were genuinely concerned about how I would manage everything. My mother-in-law's voice carried a blend of motherly love and concern as she suggested, "It's better to stay here where you have everything, all the comforts. Why struggle to start anew somewhere else?" While I sensed her concern, I also couldn't shake the feeling that there was a desire for me to struggle alone, perhaps to convince us to stay in his hometown. I might have been wrong in my assumption, but that was my feeling at the time.

Every day, frustration grew within me. I was married and had devoted my career and life to my second family and Shivam's wishes, yet I found myself questioning why he couldn't come and support me. Still, I remained determined not to give up. My skills in fashion design and teaching, along with my ability to drive, became my allies in this struggle.

Some people speculated that I had fought with my in-laws, which is why I was living with my parents. I tried to ignore their whispers, but they left a scar. Finally, we set March 31st—my birthday—as the grand opening date for our store. The interiors were nearly finished, and stock was ready. Shivam arrived on March 22nd to help settle in and start our new life.

But then, on March 23rd, the lockdown was announced. We were left in shock. For the next four to five days, we waited, hoping things would return to normal, but they didn't. On March 29th, my father-in-law sent a car to bring us back to Morena. I pleaded with my parents and Shivam to wait a few more days, at least until my first birthday after our marriage, but nothing worked. I was made to sit in the car at night, and I remember crying, feeling helpless and angry with everyone, including Shivam. All my dreams felt shattered; all my hard work seemed wasted.

During the journey back, we remained silent, but once we arrived, I forced myself to act normal, hiding my pain and disappointment. As my birthday approached, the ache of losing everything grew. My sister-in-law consoled me, saying, "That's why you shouldn't plan too far ahead." I didn't respond but went into the kitchen to make tea, tears rolling down my face as I wondered what I had done wrong to deserve this longing for a life I had worked so hard for.

My cute little niece, Pihu, caught me crying and innocently asked, "Chachi, what happened? Don't worry. Everything will be fine." She sweetly reminded me, "You have your birthday coming up! What do you want to eat?" Her heartwarming words made me cry even more, and I replied, "I don't want anything, beta, but promise you won't tell anyone that I'm crying." Clueless, she said, "Okay," while trying to make me smile.

On March 30th, I began settling into a routine and reminded myself that this was my first birthday after my marriage; I shouldn't ruin it. I resolved to accept the situation and wait a little longer. On my birthday, my niece, nephew, and sister-in-law surprised me by baking a cake and preparing a delicious meal. We enjoyed it together, but you might be wondering about Shivam's gift—that's a long story for another time. Just know that we had our first big fight after marriage.

Returning to the theme of learning, the lockdown months turned out to be advantageous. I immersed myself in baking, trying recipes that restaurants no longer offered. I spent my time sketching jewelry designs and even started an online clothing business, which turned out to be quite profitable. I taught Pihu dance, we made TikTok videos together, and I began uploading English lessons on YouTube.

Months flew by, and by August, the lockdown had lifted, though COVID-19 was still a looming concern. We finally returned to Indore. A flat owned by Shivam's family that had been rented out was now vacant. My parents ensured it was painted, furnished, and ready for us to move in. We were thrilled! The moment I imprinted my hands against the door, a sense of peace settled in my heart. My life was finally getting back on track, and the next four months became some of the best of my life. I started teaching online at our school back home. Though we hadn't inaugurated the boutique yet, we were booking exhibitions to introduce ourselves.

Soon after, I became pregnant—a new chapter was beginning, and in March, during my sixth month of pregnancy, we planned to visit my brother-in-law's roka ceremony for a week. But once again, lockdown 2.0 struck, and we found ourselves stuck. The months passed, and my estimated delivery date drew near. We made numerous attempts to return home, but obstacles kept arising. During the last two months, I became weak and ill; my hemoglobin dropped to 7. Even with iron injections and supplements every other day, I struggled to regain my strength. Countless sleepless nights ensued, but I remained determined to deliver the baby naturally, avoiding a cesarean. I walked, exercised, consumed cow ghee in milk, and tried everything I could. Every time the doctor suggested a cesarean, I reminded myself, "No, I am not weak; I will get through this."

Finally, on June 6th, our baby, Shivankh, entered our lives but I had to go through a cesarean after enduring 6 hours of labour pain. But having him in my lap made me feel as if life gave me a new purpose to dream more and work more. As I had mentioned earlier, life has a way of surprising us. What seemed like the end of my struggles and the beginning of a new life turned out to be the opposite.

One and a half months later, I found myself back at my parents' house—blank. I felt as though my heart had stopped working, leaving only my brain churning with stress about how both of us would survive. I had to manage Shivam's share market portfolio, which he had taught me about, but I was still a novice. There were lakhs of rupees owed to people, and I faced the reality of having no job, no home, no direction, and no career. People might label me as selfish, but I was caught in a turmoil, unsure whether to mourn my losses or to focus on the new life God had entrusted me with—a little life that was mine, his, and our shared responsibility and dream. Honestly, my mental health was in tatters until my cousin, Tanu, urged me to see a counselor. I knew she was right, and that suggestion became a turning point in my life. Even though I only attended a few sessions, my therapist helped me rejoin my college and resume classical dance just three months after losing Shivam. But going back to the same college where we had met and where I was now teaching was overwhelming. On my first day, I found myself running back to my car, sitting there for hours. I had several panic attacks, but somehow, I completed my semester.

For dance, I joined classes and even got certified as a Zumba instructor, eventually opening my own dance studio. Unfortunately, I couldn't sustain it for long. For delivering Shivankh, I had to undergo a cesarean operation, requiring extensive rest that I was unable to manage. My body started failing me; I developed knee and back pain, and one day, I found myself frozen in bed. The diagnosis revealed three gaps in my spine, and the doctor strictly advised against dancing. So, what now?

I pivoted to starting a Western top-selling business while simultaneously learning through online videos and managing Shivam's portfolio to recover losses. I also enrolled in a distance learning Master of Arts in Psychology program. My passion for handwriting analysis, which sparked in 12th grade, resurfaced, leading me to complete a formal graphology course. Additionally, I felt a calling to learn tarot reading, and to my surprise, my predictions were proving accurate.

Although my tops business ultimately failed, I needed a job but was not getting success in getting any as I was already late in re-entering the market. I had a son to raise, and it pained me not to be available for him 24/7—a source of guilt that haunts me to this day. Nevertheless, I decided to be practical and gave myself four years to establish a stable career, ensuring that no setback could bring me back to ground zero, at least financially. I returned to college, this time securing a full-time position as a digital marketing executive. While the job was going well, leaving my two-year-old son each morning, only to hear how much he cried or that he hadn't eaten, filled me with anxiety. So, I quit and opted for work-from-home opportunities for the next two years.

During this time, I also secured an astrology job on an online portal and launched my own venture, Mindcrafting, which I am committed to maintaining.

I know my journey is far from ideal—it's not the kind that led me straight to success (which I'll delve into in another chapter)—but it has, at the very least, kept me from hitting rock bottom during my darkest times.

At 30, I am now a psychologist, a tarot reader, numerologist, life coach, and business owner. I've realized that every skill I learned—no matter how random—served me when I needed it most. From managing businesses to teaching, from healing through dance to finding peace through astrology—everything had a purpose.

The Lesson

And here's the most important lesson: No learning is ever wasted. My life path, according to numerology, is connected to the number 3—a number that represents learning, sharing, and teaching. It makes perfect sense now.

So, if there's one thing I've learned, it's this: Keep learning, keep growing. You never know when those lessons will save you.

A Simple Exercise for Reflection

Look Back at Your Learning Journey

Reflect on your past experiences with learning and recognize the benefits they've brought to your life.

Step 1: List Your Skills and Hobbies

- Make a list of five skills or hobbies you've tried (e.g., cooking, dancing, painting, coding, or any courses).

Step 2: Explore Your Interest

- For each skill, write down:
- What sparked your interest in learning this skill?
- Any challenges or bumps along the way you faced while learning?

Step 3: Reflect on the Benefits

- Think about how each skill has positively impacted your life.
- Jot down:
- What benefits have you experienced from each skill (e.g., increased confidence, improved health, new friendships)?

Step 4: Share Your Insights

- If you're comfortable, share your reflections with a friend or family member. Discussing your journey can deepen your understanding and inspire others!

Take a moment to appreciate your learning journey. Recognizing your growth and the positive effects of your hobbies can motivate you to keep exploring new skills!

Lesson 12

Pressing the Restart Button

One afternoon, I sat in play zone in a mall while my son was trying different games with his mama, half distracted, watching a group of kids intensely focused on a PlayStation game. It was the kind of moment I could have easily ignored, just background noise in my chaotic mind. But that day, something about their playful energy drew me in. Little did I know, I was about to learn one of the most profound lessons of my life—an epiphany, disguised in the simplicity of a child's game.

Three kids were playing against each other, all eager to win, as kids usually are. But one of them kept losing, over and over again. Every time he lost, he would look a bit disheartened for a moment, but then, as if nothing had happened, he'd say, "Let's start again!" His voice carried a strange sense of hope, the kind that's undeterred by failure. I watched in amazement as this happened two, then three times. Each time, with the same unshakable enthusiasm, he restarted the game and tried again.

On the fourth try, his friends grew impatient. "Why do you even want to keep playing?" one of them teased. "You're just going to lose again! You've lost every time!"

They laughed, amused by what they saw as his foolish determination. One of them pointed to the screen and said, "Look at the score. We're way ahead of you. Even if you win the next three rounds, you'll still be behind! What's the point? Why waste your time?"

I held my breath, expecting the boy to finally give up, to feel embarrassed, or maybe angry. But instead, with a calm confidence that seemed beyond his years, he simply said, "You never know. I might win the next one. And even if I don't win, I'm having fun. Isn't that what playing is all about?"

His friends fell silent, clearly surprised by his answer. But the silence that followed hit me harder than I expected. Those words, coming from a child who had just been teased for losing, stirred something deep within me. I could feel a shift happening inside—a realization that had been long overdue.

For years, I had been trapped in a cycle of self-criticism and regret, always comparing myself to others. Everywhere I looked, people my age seemed to be winning at life. They were ticking off milestones like they were items on a shopping list: marrying the love of their lives, building stable careers, buying homes, starting families. And where was I?

I was nowhere close to those things. No husband, no stable job, no house, no financial security. I had a child who would never know the warmth of his father's presence. Life felt like a series of unfinished, broken pieces that I couldn't quite fit together. While my friends were on vacation with their partners or celebrating their careers, I was drowning in responsibilities, starting from scratch, trying to rebuild a life that had been shattered.

In the last three years, my colleagues—who started as guest lecturers just like me—had become senior faculty, secured permanent positions, earned their Ph.D.s, and some had even moved abroad. Meanwhile, I was still a guest lecturer, stuck in the same place. For a short while, I worked as a research associate, but my colleagues were people I had once taught. I watched as they surpassed me in every way, while I remained rooted to the same spot, unable to grow, unable to catch up.

And just when I thought things couldn't feel worse, I found myself at 30, working as an intern—an intern!—in an office where my supervisors and colleagues were in their early 20s. The humiliation gnawed at me every day, making me feel small, like I had somehow missed the memo on how to live life.

I sat there, still watching those kids, and something in me started to shift. That little boy, with his unwavering optimism, reminded me of something I had lost: the willingness to keep trying. He didn't care about the score. He didn't care that his friends were ahead or that they were teasing him for losing. All that mattered to him was that he was enjoying the game, and the possibility that the next round could be different.

Suddenly, my perspective shifted. The fog that had clouded my mind for so long began to lift, and I saw my life from a new angle. Instead of focusing on what I hadn't achieved, I started to see the richness of the experiences I'd had. My path hadn't been traditional or easy, but it had been mine, filled with unexpected twists and turns. I realized I had been living an adventurous life, even if it didn't look like what society deemed as "success."

Sure, I hadn't hit the typical milestones on time. I wasn't established in my career, and I hadn't followed a straight path.

But when I thought back to the psychology internship I had just completed, I realized something: For the first time in years, I felt at peace with my work. Being a school counselor had given me the satisfaction I had been searching for in all my previous jobs. It had taken me a while to get there, but I had finally found my purpose.

And then it hit me—better late than never.

I wasn't someone who wins and then sits back, comfortable in my victory. No, I was the one who kept playing, even when the odds were against me. I might not be "winning" in the traditional sense, but I was still in the game. Still trying. Still hoping. And even though I didn't know when my moment of victory would come, I knew that I would never stop trying.

That boy's words echoed in my mind, bringing a sense of peace I hadn't felt in years. I realized that life is not about winning every round. It's about staying in the game, enjoying the process, and learning from each experience. I started to reflect on my journey with a new sense of pride. No, I didn't have a husband by my side anymore, but I had known true love. The love Shivam and I shared was enough to fill my heart, even in his absence. There are people who are married but unhappy, people with partners who don't make them feel cherished. But I had been loved deeply, and that love still gave me strength.

My family might not look complete to the outside world. I was raising a child on my own, and yes, I carried a lot of responsibility on my shoulders. But I had the freedom to raise my child in my own way, and in doing so, I was becoming stronger, more resilient. And who knows? Maybe one day in my career, I might hit a jackpot. Life is full of surprises, after all.

The Lesson

Sometimes, life feels like a phone that gets stuck—frozen, unable to move forward, no matter how hard you try to make it work. After losing Shivam, my life felt like that—stuck, like I couldn't move forward no matter how much I wanted to. But just like a frozen phone, sometimes all you need to do is restart.

I'm ready to restart. I don't know what the next chapter of my life will look like, but I'm ready to play the game again. And whether I win or lose, I'll be happy knowing that I stayed in the game and enjoyed the journey.

A Simple Exercise for Reflection

Think about a time in your life when you felt "stuck" or like you were losing while everyone else seemed to be moving ahead. What was the situation, and how did it make you feel? Did you give up or keep trying?

- Now take 10 minutes to write down the "losses" or setbacks you've faced in the past few years. Next to each one, write either a *win* you gained from that experience or a *lesson* you learned. Remember, every setback carries something valuable.

Lesson 13

The Unbreakable Bonds of True Friendship

One afternoon, as I sat quietly, lost in the deep recesses of my mind, memories of countless friendships flickered like shadows on the wall. And in that moment of stillness, an undeniable truth struck me—a truth as simple as it was profound: true friendships endure. No matter the miles that separate or the years that pass, the bonds formed by the heart are unbreakable. I realized then that friendships, like rivers, are always in motion. They twist, turn, and sometimes flood our lives with warmth, even during life's harshest storms. The key lies not in how close we remain physically, but in the strength of the connection, born from mutual respect and an unshakable bond.

Friendships, like the seasons, change. Some pass through our lives briefly, leaving behind memories like fallen leaves, while others stand the test of time, as unyielding as ancient trees rooted deep within us. But the true power of friendship, I discovered, is not measured by how often we meet, how frequently we speak, or how close we live. No, the true value of friendship lies in presence—in showing up, in standing beside you when the world feels like it's crumbling and cheering you on when life is at its brightest. That is the undeniable truth I came to understand, slowly and painfully.

I told you before, didn't I? That I carried this deep, crushing belief for years—that no one really liked me. I felt invisible, trapped behind a wall of self-doubt that kept me from building the kind of deep connections others seemed to have so effortlessly. Even the friends I held close, the ones I thought were my people, I constantly wondered: Do they feel the same about me? And time after time, the answer I imagined in the quiet corners of my mind was always no. As life carried us from the halls of school to the demands of college, then jobs, marriages, and all the milestones in between, friendships faded. Communication dwindled. I watched as people came and went, and I became convinced that I had no real friends, no tribe, no circle to call my own.

Maybe that's why I never had those tight-knit friend groups you see in movies, the ones that stand by you through everything. For the most part, I drifted into Shivam's circle of friends, or I leaned on my forever girl gang from college, the ones who created our little sanctuary, the "Love Square" on WhatsApp. They were my constants, the ones who, even when I faltered, never wavered. And then, there was one other—a childhood friend, Shanu. I don't even remember how old we were when Shanu and I became friends. She's probably my oldest friend, someone I found through my parents' social circles. Despite coming from very different backgrounds—whether in terms of finances or lifestyle—she never made me feel less in any way. While others, at times, unintentionally highlighted our differences, she never saw them. With her, I could always speak my heart out, anytime, anywhere.

We don't talk as often as we used to, life having pulled us in different directions. But even now, when I have an important decision to make, she's one of the first people I call. And no matter how busy she is, she always picks up.

Before my marriage, I used to call her my *girl-boyfriend*. When Shivam was in Morena, and I needed to escape for a while, she was the one I'd turn to. After finishing her work, she'd show up around 7 or 8 in the evening, and we'd either go for a drive or just sit in the car and talk for hours. She was my safe space.

Shivam. He was magnetic. People gravitated toward him effortlessly, and his circle of friends seemed endless. Sometimes I envied that—how he could connect with others so easily, but how could I truly be jealous? He was my best friend, my partner, the one person who knew me like no one else ever would. With Shivam, I was free—free to be my most unguarded, wild self, the side of me no one else had ever seen. And to this day, I doubt anyone else ever will. He was enough for me. We shared every part of life—our secrets, our laughter, our dreams... dreams that would never come to pass.

When I lost Shivam, people said I lost a husband, but I knew the truth. That day, I lost everything—a part of my soul, my other half. And all I had left was a piece of us cradled in my lap. In those first, suffocating days, when the house was filled with people, I found myself talking endlessly about him. I relived every detail, every conversation, as if I could somehow bring him back with my words. But I was in denial. And in the rare moments of silence, the truth would creep in like a dark fog. Inside my mind, there was a movie I couldn't stop, one where I watched him slipping away from me—slowly—from our mornings, our meals, our nights spent binge-watching side by side, from the walks where his hand always rested on my shoulder. Scene by scene, he vanished from my life, until there was nothing left but memories... and emptiness. People who visited me looked confused and felt sorry for me, like they thought I'd gone crazy.

Then there were Naman and Manali. From the first moment, they stood by my side—feeding me when I couldn't eat, comforting me when I couldn't breathe. We had been inseparable in college, as couples, as friends. Those weekends we shared together? They were the happiest days of my life. After Shivam left, they did too—but not really. Though the distance grew, they never truly left me. Their calls, their texts, their unwavering assurance kept me grounded, though every word reminded me of what I had lost. And every time I heard their voices, I missed him more. How could I not? He was the missing piece in our conversations, the silence in our laughter.

During those difficult days, many old friends from college and school found their way back into my life. After years of minimal contact, their visits brought an overwhelming sense of relief, like a weight I didn't know I was carrying had suddenly been lifted. My school friends, in particular, became an unexpected pillar of strength. One friend, in particular, became my confidante—a sort of philosopher who gave me the freedom to express every raw emotion without judgment. Even with a busy life of his own, he always found the time to respond to my long, meandering messages, offering me clarity when everything felt chaotic.

And then, of course, there's my Love Square—Aishu, Akku & Nancy, my pillars. They've witnessed me in every possible state: breaking, shattering, rambling incoherently, and even pulling away into complete isolation. When everyone else gave up after countless unanswered calls, these girls held on. If I didn't pick up, they'd call my mom. If I didn't go to meet them, they'd show up at my doorstep. I stood them up more times than I care to admit—even on my birthday—but they never wavered. They're still here, holding me up, refusing to let go.

But after Shivam, Shanu wasn't around much. And it hurt—a lot. I felt like she was distancing herself from me, and I couldn't understand why. Was it because she was getting married? Did she not want my sadness to weigh on her? Had she moved on to a world of couples where I no longer fit? The thoughts were heartbreaking. I even missed her wedding, something I still regret to this day.

Later, I found out the truth—she wasn't avoiding me out of indifference, but out of her own pain. She didn't know how to face me, how to be around me in my grief. She was scared of seeing me like that, unsure of what to say or do.

Now, we've found our way back to each other. The bond remains, unchanged at its core. She often tells me, *"I never knew you were so strong."* And all I can reply is, *"Neither did I. But I didn't have a choice."*

The Lesson

Reflecting on all the friendships I've had, I see how they fit into different categories. Some friends are there for fun. Others provide advice and support during tough times, even if they don't stay forever. And then, there are the rare few who have seen me at my best and worst, yet still choose to stay.

True friendships are rare, but when they are found, they can last a lifetime. They aren't defined by how often you meet or how frequently you talk. Instead, they are measured by the strength of the bond, the willingness to forgive, and the comfort of simply being in each other's presence.

Friendship is about showing up, being present, and offering grace when it's needed. Whether it's about forgiving an old friend or learning to become your own, the journey is always worth it.

A Simple Exercise for Reflection

Take a moment to reflect on the friendships in your life. Write down answers to these questions:

1. **Who are your pillars?** - List the friends who have been with you through thick and thin. What makes these friendships special?

2. **When was the last time you expressed gratitude to them?** - Write a message or letter thanking them for their support, even if you don't send it.

3. **Identify a friendship that may need healing.** - Is there someone you've drifted from due to a misunderstanding or distance? Consider reaching out to reconnect or simply reflect on whether the friendship still serves you.

Lesson 14

The Tug-of-War Between Freedom and Loneliness

Life, for me, has become a delicate balancing act between two opposing forces—freedom and loneliness. The two emotions, though intertwined, are so different in their impact. Freedom feels exhilarating, a chance to breathe, spread my wings, and reclaim parts of myself. Loneliness, though, is heavy and suffocating, a quiet ache that refuses to leave even when I'm surrounded by the people I love.

After Shivam's passing, I was fortunate to have friends and family rally around me. My in-laws repeatedly tell me that their home is mine, always inviting me over, reminding me that I can come anytime I want. My sister-in-law checks on me regularly, asking if I need anything. My brothers-in-law have stepped up as older brothers to me, always just a phone call away if I need help with Cheeku or anything else. My cousins remind me how blessed I am to have grown up in a close-knit family. And then, of course, there are my parents. They haven't left my side for even a moment since Shivam left, taking on the role of parents again, but this time for Cheeku.

My father, for instance, brings toys for Cheeku every day, takes him to the park, on scooter rides, and to the supermarket, where they pick out chocolates and treats. He spoils him with love and affection, much to my frustration. I often scold him, telling him he's unknowingly spoiling Cheeku, to which my son cleverly retorts, "Nanu, don't listen to Mumma, let's go." And my father smiles and reassures me, "Don't worry, just let him enjoy. You'll see, he'll turn out fine."

My mother and my grandmother are my constant allies, helping me raise Cheeku. He's grown up knowing three mothers—me, his "Nani Mumma," and his "Moti Nani" (great-grandmother). They've been there every step of the way, from feeding him to bathing him, ensuring he's always cared for. Yet, because of our generational differences, we often clash in our parenting styles. I believe in a little discipline, trying to curb bad habits before they take root. My mother, however, feels his stubbornness is a result of his circumstances, believing that I'm not giving him enough attention due to my work. Then there's my grandmother, who silently observes our clashes but often encourages me to tolerate everything with patience and love.

And I can't forget Prakhar, Cheeku's beloved *mama* (maternal uncle) and my younger brother. Since Shivam left, Prakhar has become a father figure to Cheeku in every possible way. There are moments, I'll admit, when I've been too emotionally drained to give Cheeku my all, but Prakhar has never missed a beat. He has done everything—from feeding him, staying up all night to comfort him, and even cleaning his potty. Now, even though Prakhar lives in Pune, he calls every day to check in, asking about Cheeku. His love for my son is uncompromising.

So yes, I have people around me who love and care for me and my son. They have done everything they can to support me. But still, I feel this aching loneliness, this feeling of not truly belonging anywhere. Even though I'm surrounded by family, I feel like I don't have a home of my own, that I'm dependent on them for everything. This sense of not belonging gnaws at me.

People often advise me to remarry, warning me, "Life is long. It might seem manageable now, but when Cheeku grows up and leaves, you'll be all alone. Your parents and brother won't be around forever—they'll have their own lives, and you'll regret it." One lady even told me, "The world is cruel, especially for single women. Men will only take advantage of you, so it's better to settle down with someone, anyone, for your own safety."

Her words echoed in my mind, stirring up all kinds of anxiety. Yes, loneliness haunts me. I feel it every night. Sometimes I wonder if I have the strength to continue like this, to shoulder all this responsibility on my own. But the idea of marrying someone just for the sake of security terrifies me. What if I marry the wrong person? What if the relationship becomes toxic, harmful not only to me but to Cheeku too? Wouldn't that be worse than being alone?

She replied, "There will be struggles no matter what. Better to struggle with one man than to face the world alone." Though I know she meant well, her words left me feeling torn. Every day, I replay that conversation in my mind, weighing my options, fearing the future, but also fearing the loss of freedom.

It's true—I crave freedom. I often feel stifled living with my parents. At this age, having to follow their rules and hearing constant remarks about how I should parent Cheeku wears me down. I know deep down that I've done my best. It wasn't easy—nothing about this journey has been. I remember waking up on Cheeku's six-month birthday, staring at the ceiling and calculating how many more years I'd need to endure this until he was old enough to stand on his own.

Since Shivam's death, all I've wanted to do is cry. But I couldn't. I didn't. I had Cheeku to care for, so I buried my grief and did what needed to be done. It wasn't easy. I went back to work three months later, even though the mere thought of driving filled me with dread. Every bike on the road reminded me of Shivam's accident, and yet, I forced myself to keep going. I forced myself to attend social gatherings, even when being around other parents and children only intensified the ache in my heart, reminding me of what Cheeku would never have—a complete family.

For three years, I've pushed through, without joy, without motivation—only a fierce determination to give Cheeku the best life I can. But even then, I'm often told I'm not doing enough, that I'm neglecting him, that my grief is affecting him. It's heartbreaking. No matter how hard I try, it never feels like enough.

That's why I dream of freedom. A life where I don't have to ask for permission, where I'm free from the expectations of being the perfect mother or daughter. Sometimes, I just want to escape, to be free of all the weight I carry every day. I imagine a home of my own, a space where I can breathe without constantly being judged. I want to break free from the endless responsibilities and demands that come with motherhood, with family, with life.

But then, I think of Cheeku. I know that having a family around is giving him a sense of stability, a semblance of normalcy in a life that has been anything but. This constant tug-of-war between my need for freedom and my fear of loneliness consumes me. I want both, but I don't know how to have both without losing my sanity.

The friend and philosopher Priyal - I mentioned in the last lesson, my old schoolmate, gave me advice that has stayed with me every day. When we met for the first time after Shivam's passing, I found myself pouring out everything about the past seven years. He didn't ask for it, but maybe I just needed to let it all out, and he felt like a safe space. For 30-35 minutes, I spoke non-stop while he patiently listened.

When I finally paused, I asked him, "I don't know how I'm going to manage. How can I keep going? I feel like I've lost everything."

He looked at me calmly and said, "You will. I know you, and you're strong. Just take it one day at a time."

That simple sentence has been my anchor. Since then, every morning, I remind myself to just take it one day at a time.

I know I need both—freedom and family—but finding a balance between the two seems impossible right now. But maybe, just maybe, the key to peace lies somewhere between them, and that's what I hope to explore in the next chapter of my life.

The Lesson

This experience has taught me that true freedom isn't about escaping responsibility or breaking free from the bonds of family. It's about finding a balance – a harmony between the demands of life and the pursuit of personal fulfillment. It's about recognizing that independence doesn't mean isolation, and that true strength lies in navigating the complexities of life with grace and resilience.

I've learned that the love and support of family, while sometimes challenging, are invaluable. They provide a safety net, a sense of belonging, and a reminder that we are never truly alone. And while navigating these complex relationships can be difficult, the rewards far outweigh the challenges.

A Simple Exercise for Reflection

1. **Identify Opposites:** What are the two major forces pulling you in different directions? (e.g., freedom vs. responsibility, loneliness vs. connection)

2. **Evaluate Each:** What are the pros and cons of each? Why are they important to you?

3. **Assess Your Balance:** Are you leaning too much one way? What would happen if you adjusted?

4. **Create a Plan:** Make small changes to bring more balance.

5. **Take it Slow:** Don't strive for perfection overnight. Focus on small daily adjustments.

Chapter 15

The Strength in His Tiny Hands

There was a time when life felt unbearably heavy, when I stood at the edge of despair, contemplating giving up. The weight of loneliness and exhaustion crushed me, and the thought of continuing seemed pointless. Suicidal thoughts became an unwelcome but familiar shadow, whispering that there was nothing left for me in this world. But then, there was Cheeku. My little boy. My reason.

Every time my mind drifted toward darkness, there he was—his tiny eyes searching mine, filled with expectation and love. A love so pure that it made me pause. How could I take away his right to a normal childhood? How could I leave when he was looking up at me, counting on me? He deserved everything a child should have—love, security, a future. And if I gave up, what would be left of his world?

I never expected gratitude. I never expected that one day he would look back and acknowledge the choices I made or the sacrifices I endured. It wasn't about that. As Shivam once told me, our duty is to give our children the best we can, without expecting them to return the favor. Also my friend Priyal, raised by a single mother himself, always reminded me, *"Whatever you do, remember—it's your choice.*

Don't hold expectations from him. Don't let it burden him when he grows up." I took those words to heart, kept my expectations in check.

And then, as Cheeku grew, I began to truly understand the depth of my decision to hold on. He became my reason to live, my source of joy in ways I never imagined. Though surrounded by many people, when he is sick, all he wants is me. My lap. My warmth. My presence. His tiny arms wrapping around me remind me that I am irreplaceable in his world. And in those moments, I understand—life is worth it.

Despite being just three, he sees me, he understands me. When I am unwell, he becomes my little caretaker, offering me food, reminding me to take my medicines, gently massaging my head or legs with his tiny hands. It's as if he knows—knows that his presence is what keeps me going. And he does it in the smallest, most beautiful ways.

Even when I scold him, he comes to me crying, saying, *"Mumma, please hug me. Speak nicely."* And I know—he is not innocent in that moment; he has already tested my patience in every way possible. But still, he chooses me and it just melts my heart. When I leave for work, he doesn't like it, but he hugs me and says, *"Mumma, jaldi aana, dhyan rakhna."* (Mom, come back soon, take care of yourself.) He asks me how my day was, and I find myself telling him—sharing little stories about my students, about the good and the troublesome moments. Talking to him nowadays feels like talking to someone mature, someone who listens and understands beyond his years.

Sometimes, when I feel guilty for not being able to do everything for him, I tell him, *"Sorry beta, Mumma aaj tumhari favorite dish nahi bana pai ya tumhe ghumane nahi le ja pai."* (Sorry, my child, today I couldn't make your favorite dish or take you out.) And his response always melts my heart—*"Koi baat nahi Mumma, baad mein kar lenge."*

(It's okay, Mom, we'll do it later.) Such simple, selfless words, yet they carry the weight of unconditional love.

One day, after my shower, I stepped into my room and found my clothes neatly laid out on the bed, along with my creams and toiletries. A little surprise from my little boy. Beaming with pride, he looked up at me and said, *"Mumma, when I grow up, I'll bring you new lipsticks. I'll take you to new countries."* His innocent dreams for me filled my heart in ways words could never express.

He watches me closely, sensing my worries even when I try to hide them. When I'm stressed about work, when he hears me talk about money struggles, he doesn't ask questions—he simply acts. Running to fetch his little piggy bank, he offers it to me with his tiny hands, saying, *"Mumma, take all my money."* (Mom, take all my money.) At that moment, I realized—this is what unconditional love looks like. Pure, untainted, without expectations.

Cheeku knows we don't have his father around. He asks about him sometimes, wondering how we could bring him back. And each time, with a heavy heart, I tell him the truth—*"Beta, we can't."* (Son, we can't.) He listens, nods, and says, *"You are my Mumma-Papa."* (You are my Mom and Dad.) And just like that, he gives me strength. The strength to keep going, to take every leap of faith needed to ensure he has a happy, fulfilling life.

His little hands in mine, his unwavering trust, his boundless love—these are my anchors. These are my reasons to live, to fight, to believe. Because in his eyes, I see the reflection of all the love I need. And that is more than enough.

The Lesson

Life has a way of testing our resilience, but in those darkest moments, we often find our greatest sources of strength. Sometimes, our reasons to hold on are right in front of us, in the form of pure, unconditional love. I have learned that love, no matter how small or simple, has the power to heal wounds, to fill empty spaces, and to give life a new meaning. It is not about expecting anything in return, but about giving and receiving wholeheartedly, knowing that the impact of love goes beyond words.

A Simple Exercise for Reflection

Think of a time when you felt like giving up.

- What or who helped you hold on?
- What small, everyday moments bring you joy and remind you why life is worth living?
- How do you express love and gratitude to those who support you?
- Are there any expectations you hold that you might need to let go of in order to love more freely?
- If you were to write a letter to yourself, acknowledging your strength and resilience, what would you say?

Take a few moments to reflect and write down your thoughts. You might be surprised at how much strength you carry within you.

Lesson 16

Respecting Myself – A Journey of Validating

From a very young age, I've been sensitive, and I mean very sensitive. I've always felt things deeply, even the tiniest of slights. While some might brush things off as trivial, for me, they lingered—gnawing at my heart and mind. For years, people around me dismissed my emotions, labeling me as "too sensitive," "overdramatic," or worse, "negative."

"You misunderstand everything," they'd say. "You blow things out of proportion." Their words would cut me deeply, as if my feelings were invalid just because they didn't see the world the way I did. This dismissal was gaslighting at its finest, and for years, I questioned myself: Were they right? Was I just overreacting?

It took years of emotional turmoil and countless incidents to accept the truth: my feelings are valid. What seems small to others may feel monumental to me—and that's okay. But that self-acceptance came at a cost, one paved with painful experiences.

I've always valued my belongings deeply, not just for their material worth but because of what they symbolized. Growing up in a middle-class family, nothing came easy. Every small thing—a new dress, a pair of earrings, or even a school notebook—came with a story of effort, compromise, and sacrifice.

Take, for example, my aversion to sharing footwear. In class 6, I developed a severe fungal infection in my toenail—a grotesque, painful ordeal that turned my nail black and left white growths spreading like unwelcome invaders. Visits to the doctor became routine, and every trip was punctuated by pain and embarrassment, especially during dance classes or anywhere I had to remove my socks.

One day, I worked up the courage to ask the doctor:

"Why me? I keep my feet clean, I bathe daily. Why did this happen to me?"

His answer changed my life:

"You might have worn someone else's footwear, or maybe someone else wore yours and passed the infection to you."

That was it. I decided then and there: *Never again.* Never would I share footwear, nor would I let others use mine. It wasn't just about hygiene—it was about self-preservation, protecting myself from unnecessary pain.

My attitude toward sharing clothes was shaped differently but just as powerfully. My mother, a graceful woman who rarely indulged herself, once participated in a fashion show. She had her heart set on a stunning black georgette suit, adorned with intricate pearl handwork. It was costly, far beyond what we could comfortably afford, but she eventually bought it after much deliberation. The day we purchased it, I saw the worry in her eyes—a mix of guilt and longing. That dress symbolized more than just fashion; it was her way of saying, *I'm trying to compete, to belong.*

I, too, cherished that suit, guarding it like a treasure. It wasn't just fabric; it was a piece of my mother's dream and sacrifice. Imagine my heartbreak when my mother, ever generous, lent it to an acquaintance. Despite my protests, she insisted it was selfish to refuse. Days later, the suit came back ruined—shrunk beyond repair. My chest felt heavy with anger and despair. I couldn't stop the tears as I held the damaged dress in my hands, blaming my mother for not respecting my feelings.

"I told you not to lend it out! What was the need?" I cried.

Her reply stung like a slap: "You're so selfish. You need to learn to share."

Was I selfish? Maybe. But that incident reinforced my belief: *Some things are too precious to share.*

Years later, this same mindset led to conflicts in my married life. I had barely settled into my new role as a bride when I realized my in-laws had different expectations about sharing. One day, guests arrived—close family friends of my in-laws—and casually began asking to borrow my new sarees and jewelry.

I felt trapped. Denying them outright felt rude, but sharing my things, especially items with sentimental value, felt like betraying myself. I quietly told my sister-in-law in the kitchen, "Bhabhi, I don't like sharing my things. I had a fungal infection once, and since then, I've been very particular." I hoped she'd understand and redirect their attention, but to my horror, she did the opposite—offering even my diamond jewelry.

As soon as the guests left, I burst into tears and confronted Shivam.

"When I've made my boundaries clear, why can't you or your family respect them?" I asked, my voice trembling with frustration.

What followed was a heated argument. Shivam, the man who had always supported my individuality, accused me of being selfish and disrespectful. His words cut deep, leaving a wound I didn't know how to heal.

That fight marked a turning point in my life. For the first time, I realized that even those who love you deeply can fail to understand your feelings. Love doesn't always guarantee empathy; sometimes, perceptions and priorities clash.

But it was also the moment I decided to stand my ground. If my boundaries, preferences, and emotions were going to be labeled selfish, so be it. I wasn't going to apologize for who I was anymore. My feelings—however "small" they seemed to others—were important to me, and I refused to let anyone invalidate them.

The Lesson

Through these experiences, I learned that **respecting myself isn't selfish—it's essential. Boundaries aren't walls; they're safeguards for our mental and emotional well-being.** Whether it's not sharing footwear, protecting sentimental items, or refusing to accommodate others at the cost of my comfort, these choices reflect my values and my right to be true to myself.

Today, I don't flinch when someone calls me "too sensitive" or "selfish." Those words no longer define me. What matters is that I've learned to honor my feelings, set boundaries, and demand respect—not just from others but also from myself.

This journey hasn't been easy. It's been filled with tears, arguments, and moments of doubt. But it's also brought me clarity: **My feelings matter. My preferences matter. I matter. And no one, not even those I love most, has the right to make me feel otherwise.**

A Simple Exercise for Reflection

Take a quiet moment to yourself. Grab a notebook or journal and write down the answers to the following prompts:

- Think of a recent situation where you felt hurt, dismissed, or invalidated. What happened, and how did it make you feel?
- Did you express your feelings in that moment? If not, what stopped you? If yes, how were your feelings received?
- On a scale of 1-10, how much weight did you give to your own emotions compared to how others perceived the situation?

Lesson 17

My Oath

It was a particularly rainy week. The kind of rain that makes the roads slick and the schoolyards muddy, forcing unexpected holidays upon everyone. The school grounds were muddy, and students trudged through puddles, their shoes caked with dirt. Inside, the dampness lingered, but it didn't dampen the spirit of the children. The hallways buzzed with chatter and laughter as they recounted their unexpected rain-filled holidays.

I was scheduled to conduct a group therapy session with a few sixth-grade students that day. Among them was a boy who had always caught my attention. He was one of those children whose presence you couldn't ignore—not because he was loud or demanding but because there was a quiet depth to him. One moment, he'd light up the room with his lively energy, and the next, he'd retreat into his thoughts, as if wrestling with a world only he could see.

The session began as usual. I encouraged the children to share stories about their rainy-day adventures, and their voices filled the room with anecdotes of laughter and joy. One girl animatedly described her visit to her family's farmhouse, her eyes sparkling with excitement. Another boy talked about a cozy movie night with his family, while a third child boasted about his mom's special paneer curry, which had become the highlight of their celebration.

It was at this moment that the boy, the one who intrigued me, spoke up. "Paneer? What's that?" he asked, his voice innocent and genuinely curious.

The room fell silent for a beat before erupting into laughter. "You don't know what paneer is?" one child teased. "Then what do you eat on special occasions?"

His cheeks flushed, but he managed a nervous smile. "Special fruits," he replied, his voice soft but steady. "My father is a fruit vendor. He brings home expensive fruits whenever we want to celebrate something."

The other children, still giggling, pressed further. "So, you've never tasted paneer?"

He looked down, his fingers fidgeting with the edge of his notebook. "No," he admitted quietly.

I quickly stepped in to change the topic, steering the conversation back to safer ground. But the boy's words lingered with me long after the session ended. As I drove home that evening, the rain tapping gently against my windshield, my mind replayed the scene over and over. His innocent question, his nervous smile, and the pride in his voice as he spoke of his father's fruits—it all left a mark on me.

At home, I watched my son push his plate away, leaving half-eaten chunks of paneer untouched. "I don't feel like eating this today," he said, sliding off his chair to go play. I sighed, shaking my head as I packed the leftovers into the fridge. Paneer—a source of protein, a staple in so many households—was just another mundane dish for him. Yet, for that boy in school, it was an unknown luxury. My mind wandered back to the boy's words about celebrating with fruits, about the joy he found in something as simple as his father's offerings.

That evening, as I sat in my room, I felt a wave of gratitude wash over me. Despite the struggles I often lamented about, I had the privilege of putting a variety of dishes on my family's table. My son could afford to be picky, leaving food untouched simply because he didn't feel like eating it. But there were children who celebrated life with fruits, cherishing what they had with a purity that was both humbling and inspiring.

In Jainism, the faith I was raised in, there is a profound emphasis on taking "niyam"—a vow or an oath that brings discipline and meaning to one's life. Many people take niyam to abstain from certain foods, like potatoes, or to dedicate themselves to fasting and prayers. That night, I decided to take a niyam of my own. But it wasn't about abstaining from a particular food or following a ritual. Instead, it was about changing the way I conducted myself as a human being.

I vowed never to bargain with fruit or vegetable vendors. It was a small gesture, but one that carried immense significance for me. These vendors, often standing under the scorching sun or braving the pouring rain, are not just selling produce—they are supporting their families. For them, the extra 40 or 50 rupees we haggle over could mean the difference between affording a basic necessity or going without. Yet, we often waste that same amount on frivolities without a second thought.

The memory of that boy and his pride in his father's fruits solidified my resolve. If my niyam could contribute even a little to their dignity, it was worth it. And in doing so, I hoped to instill the same values in my son—to teach him that privilege comes with a responsibility to be kind, compassionate, and fair.

The Lesson

Life has a way of teaching us profound lessons in the most ordinary moments. That day, amidst the chatter and laughter of schoolchildren, I was reminded of the importance of gratitude and empathy. The boy's innocent question about paneer opened my eyes to the silent struggles and joys of others. It taught me to look beyond my own world and to appreciate the simple, often overlooked blessings in life.

Gratitude isn't about the grand gestures or the big wins—it's about finding joy in the ordinary, about recognizing the privilege we often take for granted. And empathy? It's about understanding that everyone has a story, one that deserves kindness and respect.

A Simple Exercise for Reflection

- Empathy Challenge: The next time you interact with someone in a service role—a fruit vendor, a cab driver, or even a waiter—pause and think about their story. Imagine the effort they put into their work and the challenges they might face. Instead of bargaining or complaining, offer a kind word, a smile, or even a little extra payment as a token of appreciation. Notice how this act of empathy not only uplifts them but also leaves you with a sense of connection and warmth.
- Mindful Spending Reflection: For one week, track your daily expenses. At the end of each day, reflect on how much of your spending was on necessities versus luxuries. Identify one area where you can reduce unnecessary spending and redirect that money toward a meaningful cause—like giving a generous tip to a vendor or buying something small for someone in need.

Lesson 18

Siblings Are Your Lifeline

Often, we hear about sibling rivalry as people grow up, but in my case, my siblings have been nothing short of blessings. They are my lifelines—my pillars of strength, my safety nets, and the foundation of my happiness. If I were to summarize my life's most profound relationships, it would all lead back to my siblings and the enduring bonds we've shared.

Growing up, my relationship with Prakhar was a beautiful mix of shared responsibilities and quiet understanding. While I was the elder one who often took charge, he was the silent observer who always had my back. We didn't fight over silly things like most siblings; instead, we instinctively cared for each other. Whether it was him ensuring I had my favorite food waiting after school or me helping him through the challenges of childhood, there was a sense of unspoken teamwork. And whenever I faced a tough situation, Prakhar stood tall, ready to defend me, no questions asked.

Even as a child, he seemed to sense things no one else did. My mom used to say he was scared of my temper and tantrums and would do everything to make sure I didn't get upset. I'd like to believe it wasn't just fear but a quiet understanding of me that made him so thoughtful. I still remember coming home from school and seeing him checking with the cook about the food. "Didi ke liye khaana bacha hai na? Usko pasand hoga na?" He knew I had a long list of likes and dislikes back then, and despite being the younger one, he took it upon himself to make sure I was happy.

Even though he was so caring, there was a part of me that felt unseen. Looking back, I now realize how he might have sensed the silent hurt I carried as a child. My parents, busy with financial struggles and adjusting to a new city, seemed to remember every tiny detail about his childhood—his first word ("phapphu," which became a family joke), his favorite dishes, and even his little quirks. But when it came to my milestones, their memories were a blur.

One day, I asked my mom, "Mumma, what was my first word? Who did I play with the most when I was a baby?" She sighed and said, "Beta, I don't remember. Those were tough times for us. Your papa and I were struggling to build a life here in Indore. Honestly, we didn't even realize when you grew up."

That reply hit me hard. It wasn't Prakhar's fault, of course, but it made me feel like I didn't matter as much. I'd wonder, "Is it because I'm not as calm and sweet as him? Is that why they only remember my tantrums and anger?"

There were days when my frustration would boil over.

"Why do you always remember what he likes—rajma, bhindi—but never remember that I hate gobhi or baingan? Why?" I'd ask angrily. My parents would just brush it off, saying I was jealous of him.

I used to worry that even Prakhar might think I was jealous, but deep down, I hoped he understood. I wasn't competing with him. I wasn't fighting for what was his. I was just fighting for what was equally ours.

When he left for college, I cried like a baby while packing his things. I bought him branded jeans and a nice watch, hoping he'd feel confident and never out of place. But in my heart, I knew things would never be the same. We wouldn't share the same home, the same routines. That chapter of our lives was over.

After I got married, I noticed how he started sharing more with my parents or even Shivam than with me. It made me happy to see their bond grow, but a small part of me wondered, "Does he still think I'm scary? Is that why he doesn't call me when he's in trouble? Is he even emotionally attached to me?"

But it wasn't until adulthood, when life threw its harshest challenges at me, that I truly understood the depth of our bond.

June 14, 2021, was one such day—a day that shattered me. That day turned my world upside down. I was in a room full of people, crying uncontrollably, unable to make sense of anything. And there he was, standing at the door. I rushed to him and hugged him tight—probably for the first time ever. We cried together, and he whispered, "Didi, sab sambhal lenge apan."

Those words were my lifeline. In that moment, I knew I could trust him with everything.

For the next few months, my siblings became my entire support system. Prakhar, my cousins, everyone stepped in to make sure I wasn't alone. They did everything to make me feel supported. They shopped for Cheeku's clothes and toys, celebrated his milestones, and captured every little moment to make sure nothing was missed.

Prakhar, especially, went above and beyond. He would wake up all night to make sure Cheeku didn't cry. If I had to rush to the doctor, Yash was just a call away. Prashu was always there for Cheeku during those scary vaccination appointments. He knew Cheeku got a bit freaked out by the needles, so he'd be right by his side, making sure he felt safe. As a reward for being such a brave boy, they'd always celebrate with a special treat – a delicious pastry from his favorite bakery. It was their little tradition, and Cheeku always looked forward to it. Yashi was the one aunt Cheeku would seek out for board game battles. Her enthusiasm for these encounters seemed less about the games and more about finding an excuse to spend time with him. Her emotions surrounding Cheeku were intense – she even confessed to crying after a dream where she slapped him. When it came to Cheeku, she'd seize any opportunity to see him, almost as if he were a famous star. She was also my steadfast companion during a crucial trip to Goa, which played a significant role in my emotional recovery. Infact all his aunt's - Manya, Khushi, Kuhu, Yashi, Tashi, and Tanu took turns playing with him, feeding him healthy food, and teaching him rhymes. Whenever Khushi and Kuhu are around, I can relax knowing he's in good hands. They have a magical way of ensuring he eats, even when he's faced with a plate of those dreaded 'healthy' vegetables. It can take him forever to finish them, but somehow, they cajole him into taking each bite. They're also the water police, making sure he stays hydrated throughout the day. Kuhu, especially, becomes his playful partner-in-crime. Their laughter echoes through the house, a constant reminder of the joy they bring to his life. And Kinshu—he was always there, keeping an eye on Cheeku at events, never letting him out of his sight, ensuring I could breathe freely.

Prakhar never thought twice about what Cheeku needed. Budget was never a concern; all that mattered to him was that whatever he got for Cheeku was the best—just like Shivam would've wanted. He often said, "I have to work harder and earn more so that Cheeku gets the life Jiju dreamed of." And even, Prakhar's wife, Kratika, is a total lifesaver! Somehow, she managed to convince Cheeku to actually go to school regularly, something we thought was impossible. Now, he eagerly awaits their evening video calls, pouring out his heart about his day and, of course, trying his best to charm her into getting him a gift. Kratika, bless her heart, always makes time for him, even when she's busy. And she's a master at motivating him – those little gifts she sends are like magic, encouraging him to be a better boy.

Even during Prakhar's wedding, when I worried about handling my little tornado of energy, my siblings didn't let me stress for even a moment. He was timely fed by one his mama's or masi's. Manya made sure Cheeku was bathed and dressed every morning, and everyone kept an eye on him in the crowd so I could enjoy the festivities without worry.

I even once stressed about how I'd raise Cheeku alone as my siblings got busy with their own lives. Manya laughed and said, "Didi, don't worry. We're so many of us! We'll take turns helping you. By the time the youngest of us gets married, Cheeku will already be grown up." Her words gave me so much relief.

Prakhar's wife, Kratika, is no less of a blessing. She always reassures me, "Didi, live your life the way you want. Don't stress about earning or a second marriage. We're here for you and Cheeku—always." And honestly, her words are a balm to my soul. Even in the little things, like her conversations with Cheeku, I can sense her genuine care and love for him. She has this way of making me believe that no matter what, my son is surrounded by people who will love and protect him just as I would.

Even in moments of uncertainty, I know one thing for sure—Cheeku will never lack love or care. With siblings like mine, how could he? They are my biggest blessing and proof that the Indian way of family—this collectivism—isn't just a tradition; it's the foundation of true happiness.

The Lesson

These moments have taught me something invaluable: the power of family, of collectivism. Growing up, our parents always emphasized staying close, supporting each other, and putting family first. Back then, it sometimes felt like a burden. But today, I see the beauty and strength in it. I have learned that true happiness and resilience come from the collective support of family. It is this foundation of love and togetherness that gives us the strength to face life's challenges and celebrate its joys. The bonds we share with our siblings and family are what keep us grounded, nurtured, and uplifted, no matter what life throws our way. The Indian way of family isn't just a tradition; it's the essence of our happiness and well-being.

A Simple Exercise for Reflection

Write a heartfelt letter to each of your siblings or family members, expressing your appreciation, love, and gratitude. Reflect on how each person has contributed to your life and what they mean to you.

Lesson 19

The Hidden Cost of Sympathy

I was 17 when I lost my maternal aunt to cancer. Her passing was sudden and cruel—she lived only five or six months after her diagnosis. She left behind three children: Tanu, 11, Tashi, 8, and Kinshu, who was just a year and six months old. It was the first time I had experienced death so closely. Until then, I thought life would always keep my loved ones intact. A day before she passed, she was in my room, casually asking about my future plans, helping me arrange my clothes, and laughing about small things. By the next morning, she was gone.

Her absence hit the family like a storm. It was as though someone had pulled the ground from beneath our feet. In her final months, she had prepared us for this inevitability, though we didn't realize it at the time. She would tell me little details about her children—what they liked, how they behaved, what comforted them. She taught me her signature recipe for *sev ki sabzi*, a dish everyone loved, as though passing down a piece of her heart.

Looking back, I now recognize the fear she hid behind her calm demeanor. She was preparing us for life without her. Her quiet strength planted a seed in me—a lesson I wouldn't fully grasp until years later:

that love is about empowering others, not making them dependent on your absence. She would ask me to feed little Kinshu, soothe Tashi's tantrums, or just be there for Tanu, who, despite being the eldest, was still a child herself. My aunt seemed to know Tanu would grow up too quickly after she was gone, sacrificing her own needs to care for her siblings. And that's exactly what happened.

After my aunt passed, Tanu didn't cry—not even a single tear. She put on a brave face and took on responsibilities far beyond her years. She became the mother her siblings needed, the emotional anchor for her father, and the silent support for everyone else. But her grief didn't vanish; it simmered beneath the surface, showing up as anger and frustration. Most people couldn't see it, but I did. Every time someone pitied her or her siblings, her expression hardened. It was as if their sympathy was a reminder of her helplessness, forcing her to relive the tragedy.

That's when I began to question whether pity, though well-meaning, does more harm than good. Instead, it makes people feel small, as if they're defined by their loss. My mother stepped in to fill the void my aunt left behind, pouring all her love and energy into the children. Her intentions were pure, and I respect them now, but as a teenager, I felt abandoned.

I was already sharing my mother's attention with her work, my father, my younger brother, and her business. Now, with these three kids added to the mix, I felt like I was slipping further down her list of priorities. One incident remains etched in my memory. I had a terrible headache one day and was lying in my mother's lap, seeking comfort. Suddenly, Tashi came crying. My mom asked me to get up and took Tashi into her lap instead. It felt like a dagger to my heart. These moments piled up, and my resentment grew—not towards the kids, but towards my mother for what felt like neglect.

When my parents scolded me, accusing me of jealousy or selfishness, it cut even deeper. I wasn't jealous of the kids; I loved them. I just didn't know how to articulate my feelings of loss and displacement. Anger became my shield, my only way to cope.

Despite my frustration, I worried about the kids and their future. I would tell my mom, "Don't spoil them too much. Don't let them grow up thinking their loss makes them entitled to favors." I believed that constant pity would make them dependent and weak, unable to face life's challenges. Instead, I wanted them to grow up strong and resilient, treated like any other child. But my concerns were often misunderstood. My mom thought I didn't want her to care for them, which wasn't true. This misunderstanding made me withdraw further. My fear was that this constant pity and extra attention would create an expectation in them, a feeling that the world owed them something because of their loss. I saw how easily people slipped into treating them differently, lowering expectations, excusing bad behavior, always ready with a sympathetic ear and a helping hand, even when it wasn't truly needed. For example, years later, even small requests directed at them felt loaded with this unspoken obligation. Imagine Tanu, now a young woman, trying to set boundaries with a family friend who had been so "supportive" after her mom died. The friend asks her to run an errand, something that's really inconvenient, and when Tanu hesitates, the friend's smile just... falters. Just for a second. But it's enough. That little flicker of disappointment, that unspoken "after all I did for you and your siblings," hangs in the air. It's not said outright, but it's there. It's like the pity they received as children became a kind of currency, a debt they were expected to repay indefinitely.

Years later, life came full circle. My husband, Shivam, passed away when our son, Cheeku, was just eight days old. This time, those same kids—now grown up—became my pillars of strength. Tanu, who had carried so much responsibility after her mother's passing, stepped up once again. She juggled college, work, and her own life to care for Cheeku. She fed him, cleaned him, and celebrated his monthly milestones as if he were her own. She was also the one who pushed me to go to therapy when I felt like giving up.

Tashi wrote me a letter that I will treasure forever. She reminded me of how we had cared for her after her mother's death, how I had told her that her mom was watching over her from heaven. "Now it's my turn," she wrote. "I will be there for Cheeku, just like you were there for us. Jiju left us with this responsibility, and we'll never let you down."

Kinshu, the baby I once cradled, would play his Casio and sing for me, trying to distract me from my grief and bring a smile to my face. Their love and support were pure, untainted by pity. It wasn't about what I had lost—it was about what we still had.

One day, my brother, in his thoughtful yet candid way, said, 'Maybe this is karma coming full circle, offering you a lesson.' His words landed heavily, a reminder of my past frustrations and unresolved guilt. At first, I felt defensive, but as I sat with his remark, I began to see the wisdom in it. Life often has a way of making us confront the lessons we once failed to learn. Life often offers us a chance to reflect and grow. I began to wonder if my earlier frustrations with my mother and the children had unknowingly hurt them. If so, perhaps my current struggles were a lesson in humility and understanding. I know I never hated them, but I accepted his view because maybe, unknowingly, I had hurt them. And if that's true, then perhaps Cheeku is bearing the brunt of my mistakes. That thought haunts me. It makes me want to say, "I'm sorry." To those kids, and especially to Cheeku, for any pain my actions may have caused.

This journey has taught me that pity comes with a price, one I'm unwilling to pay. I have learned—and hope to teach Cheeku—that while asking for help is not a sign of weakness, accepting pity is like inviting others to define you by your wounds. I remember, thirteen days after Shivam's passing, I stood in front of his photograph and told his brother, "I know you all want to help, and I appreciate it. But I don't want financial support or jobs offered out of sympathy. I will take time, but I will become independent. All I need from you is emotional support and the assurance that if I stumble, you'll be there to help me back up."

I've come to hate the label "bechari" (poor thing). After Shivam's death, when I first went for a walk, the women in my neighborhood either avoided me or looked at me with pity in their eyes. Their stares made me feel smaller, weaker. That's when I decided: I would never let pity define me or my son.

People offered me jobs, but I turned them down if I sensed they were given out of pity. Here's the thing about humans: when we do even the smallest favor for someone, we often expect gratitude—and not just a polite thank you, but sometimes a lifetime of indebtedness. Help should come from a place of genuine care, not from a desire for recognition or payback. Gratitude is important, but when help comes with unspoken strings, it can weigh you down. For instance, someone offered to babysit Cheeku "out of sympathy" after Shivam passed. While I appreciated the offer, I also sensed an expectation – not explicitly stated, but definitely felt – that I would forever be indebted to this person, always available to return the favor, even if it was inconvenient for me. It wasn't just about babysitting; it was about a power dynamic created by the initial act of pity-driven help. It made it harder to say no to future requests, even unreasonable ones, because of that unspoken string of obligation.

I've come to believe that showing your wounds to the world invites both healing and harm. While empathy uplifts, pity diminishes. As I reflect on these experiences, I'm learning to wear a shield of dignity—not to hide my pain, but to protect my self-worth. And that's a lesson I hope Cheeku carries forward: that strength comes not from avoiding struggles but from rising above them, with grace and gratitude intact.

The Lesson

Pity often undermines the strength and dignity of the person it's directed toward. True support uplifts without expecting anything in return. Strength comes from embracing challenges with resilience and seeking help only when it is offered with genuine care.

A Simple Exercise for Reflection

- Think about a time when you accepted help. Was it offered out of genuine care or pity? How did it make you feel?
- Reflect on how you offer help to others. Do you expect gratitude or recognition? How can you ensure your support empowers rather than diminishes?
- Write down three ways you can strengthen your own resilience without depending on others' approval or sympathy.

Lesson 20

Transforming Pain into Purpose

The day I lost Shivam felt like the ground beneath me had crumbled, leaving me suspended in an endless freefall. My heart, mind, and soul were consumed by relentless questions—questions that clawed at my sanity. "Why did this happen?" "How could it happen?" "Was it my fault?" And the most haunting of all: "Could it have been prevented?"

Shivam and I had always believed in the stars. Before our marriage, we sought guidance from astrologers, who reassured us with glowing predictions. A 32/36 gun match—nearly perfect. They acknowledged there might be struggles in the early years of our marriage but promised brighter days ahead. "After two years, and especially after a child," one astrologer assured, "his time will improve dramatically. The stars favor him post-March 2021." We clung to their words like lifelines. Mantras, pujas, donations, fasts—we did it all, believing we were safeguarding our future. But none of it mattered.

Shivam was gone, and with him went the dreams we had so carefully built. And then came the whispers—cruel, cutting whispers that shattered my already fragile world. "Maybe it was the child's destiny," some murmured. "He was born under Mool Nakshatra, you know. That nakshatra could have caused his father's death." The words landed like a physical blow, knocking the air from my lungs.

I looked at my son—my innocent baby, the only part of Shivam I had left. His tiny chest rose and fell in sleep, his delicate fingers curled into soft fists. How could anyone suggest he was to blame?

Anger burned through my grief like wildfire. I wanted answers—real answers.

I sat on the bed, my tears soaking the same gown I had worn for Shivam's funeral rites, my fingers tightening around my phone. And one by one, I called every astrologer we had ever trusted.

"Why didn't you warn us?" I demanded. "If this was destiny, why did you tell us to marry quickly? Why tell us to have a child if you knew this could happen?"

Their responses were a tangled mess of contradictions. One said a specific puja had been missed. Another labeled it an "untimely death" that no one could have foreseen. Others offered vague, evasive answers, hiding behind the excuse of divine will. None of it made sense.

As if losing Shivam wasn't enough, the people around me wouldn't give me a straight answer about how he died. All I got was a single word: accident. But accidents don't just happen. There are events, moments, and decisions that lead to them. I wasn't asking for a miracle; I was asking for clarity, for the truth. But everyone, claiming to protect me, only deepened the void with their silence. They refused to show me news reports, refused to let me speak to those who were with him in his final moments. "It's for your own good," they said. But was it? Wasn't I entitled to know what really happened in those fifteen minutes? Instead, all I was left with were gaps, doubts, and sleepless nights spent playing out every possible scenario in my mind.

Grief has a way of consuming you, of making every minute feel like an eternity. I needed answers, so when the living failed to give me answers, I turned to the universe itself.

And so, I embarked on a journey that was equal parts desperate and determined. I dove headfirst into astrology, numerology, tarot, and every spiritual science I could find. I wasn't just studying; I was searching. Searching for the "why." Why did this happen? Was it written in the stars? Was it karmic? Was there anything I could have done differently? As I immersed myself in these studies, the answers I found were not the ones I expected—but they were the ones I needed. Birth and death, I learned, are beyond prediction. They are tied to karma, the unseen thread that connects our actions to their consequences. The planets and stars don't control us; they merely reflect the energy we've put into the universe. Remedies, pujas, and rituals? They aren't magic fixes. They're tools to balance our karmic scales, to create more good energy that can soften the blow of our past mistakes.

But some lessons are meant to transform us, not just soften the blow.

Jainism taught me that every soul carries its own karmic burden. Shivam's journey was his own, shaped by forces beyond my control. His departure was not the fault of a nakshatra, or a missed ritual, or even a decision we made. It was part of his path.

And perhaps the hardest truth of all: my suffering was not a punishment—it was an awakening.

The principle of **anekantavada** (multiple perspectives) reminded me that no single truth could explain Shivam's loss. His passing was not just an event; it was a culmination of countless actions, choices, and karmic ties from this life and possibly past lives.

Jainism speaks of aparigraha—non-attachment. And wasn't attachment the reason I was suffering?

I wasn't just mourning Shivam. I was mourning the future I had imagined with him.

The life we were supposed to have. The old beliefs I had clung to. The certainty that if I did everything right, I could protect the people I loved.

But true love is not about possession. It is about release.

This truth isn't confined to Jainism or astrology. Psychology, spirituality, and other religious teachings echo the same wisdom.

- **Hinduism** speaks of karma and dharma, guiding us to act righteously while accepting the results as divine will.
- **Christianity** emphasizes forgiveness, faith, and resilience in the face of trials, teaching that suffering often carries hidden blessings.
- **Buddhism** centers around mindfulness and detachment, urging us to break free from the cycle of suffering.
- **Psychology** focuses on resilience, emotional processing, and mindful detachment, offering tools to rebuild ourselves after loss.

I had a choice. I could let my grief consume me, or I could turn it into something greater.

And so, I made a decision:

If life had stripped me of my sense of security, I would find purpose in the uncertainty.

If pain had shattered me, I would use it to help others rebuild.

I was no longer searching for answers. I was searching for a way forward.

And in doing so, I found my calling.

I didn't just study astrology, numerology, psychology, and spirituality. I started using them to guide others—to help them make sense of their own struggles, their own heartbreaks, their own unanswered questions.

My pain had become my compass. And through it, I had found my purpose.

The Lesson

Here's the most important lesson: life is about acceptance. The pain, the joy, the heartbreak, the healing—it's all part of a grander design, a cosmic script written by our own actions, thoughts, and intentions.

Shivam's loss broke me, but it also built me. It forced me to confront questions I had never asked before and to seek answers in places I had never explored. And while I may never fully understand why he was taken from me, I've come to accept that some answers are not meant to be found. Instead, they're meant to teach us to trust the journey, to honor the lessons, and to hold onto hope—even when the stars seem to betray us.

The universe has its reasons, but it also gives us tools to navigate its mysteries. Whether you turn to astrology, Jainism, psychology, or spirituality, the message is the same: trust in the process, embrace the lessons, and never stop searching for the light—even in the darkest of times.

A Simple Exercise for Reflection

Materials Needed:

- A blank sheet of paper
- Colored pens or pencils

Steps:

1. **Draw Your Life Map**

    - Draw a large circle on the paper. Divide it into eight segments, like a pie chart.
    - Label each segment with key areas of your life (e.g., Relationships, Career, Health, Spirituality, Personal Growth, Emotional Well-being, Hobbies, and Social Connections).

2. **Evaluate Each Segment**

    - Using a scale of 1 to 10, shade each segment to represent your current satisfaction or fulfillment in that area (1 being the lowest and 10 being the highest).
    - Reflect on why some areas are fuller than others.

3. **Connect to the Cosmic and Personal**

    - Think of each segment as influenced by the karmic energies you're emitting. Write a few sentences or bullet points beside each segment, identifying what thoughts, actions, or patterns might be affecting it.

- For example: If the "Relationships" segment is low, consider whether attachment, unresolved conflicts, or unspoken expectations are contributing.

4. **Identify Action Steps**

- For each segment, brainstorm one small action to enhance fulfillment or growth in that area.
- Example: For "Spirituality," you might commit to five minutes of daily meditation or reading a verse from a sacred text.

5. **Create Affirmations**

- Write a personalized affirmation for each area to inspire positive change.
- Example: For "Emotional Well-being," your affirmation could be: "I release the past and embrace the healing power of love and acceptance."

6. **Symbolic Release**

- Choose one area where you feel particularly stuck. On a separate piece of paper, write down the thoughts, fears, or regrets holding you back.
- Fold the paper and symbolically release it—burn it safely, tear it up, or bury it. This act represents letting go and making space for new energy.

7. **Revisit and Reflect**

- Revisit your Life Map weekly or monthly to track changes, reassess your fulfillment levels, and adjust your action steps.

Lesson 21

The Elusive Pursuit of Happiness

In the vast tapestry of our lives, one theme runs through every single story—the search for happiness. It's that one thing we all chase from the moment we take our first breath, hoping to find joy and fulfillment along the way. It's not just about basic needs, like food, water, or shelter. Those things are important, yes, but they're just the beginning. After those needs are met, we start to reach for something deeper, something that feels just beyond our grasp.

We begin to believe that happiness comes from things we can touch or acquire: a stable career, money, love, adventure. So we work hard for them, thinking that once we have it all, we'll finally feel happy. But here's the paradox: Even when we have everything we thought we needed, happiness still feels like a distant dream. You know the feeling—"I have a great job, a wonderful partner, a beautiful family, yet something feels missing. Why am I not happy?"

I know this feeling all too well. People often attributed my own melancholic haze to the tragic loss of my husband, Shivam. They assumed my grief, a gaping wound in my soul, was the sole culprit. "You'll get over it," they'd say, their well-intentioned words sounding hollow. "Time heals all wounds." But the truth, I realized, was far more complex. What I realized, after much reflection, is that my search for happiness didn't start with his loss. It started long before that. Even when I had everything—a circle of caring friends, loving parents, success in school, and a partner I adored—there was always this underlying sense of yearning.

I remember this one day—before the tragedy struck—sitting with Shivam at our favorite café, chatting about the future. "We've got everything we ever dreamed of, right?" I had said, watching the sunlight filter through the trees around us. He smiled, that quiet smile he always had, and said, "It feels like we do, but does it feel enough?"

I didn't have an answer for that then. But in hindsight, I think he was onto something. Happiness isn't just about having what you think you need—it's about feeling fulfilled in a way that nothing external can give you.

When Shivam passed away, I found myself surrounded by people who cared, a child who depended on me, a career I loved, a house, a car, and all the material comforts anyone could wish for. But something was still missing. People would say, "At least you have all of this. You should be thankful." I knew they meant well, but I couldn't shake the feeling that none of these things could fill the hole left by Shivam's absence. I wasn't grieving just because he was gone—I was grieving because he was supposed to be here, beside me, witnessing our life together. That's what I missed.

There was a time when I thought happiness came from things—like the material world somehow holding the key to peace. But, in truth, sometimes happiness is simply embodied by a person. That person becomes the safe harbor in the storm of life. I took Shivam's presence for granted when he was here. His laugh, his way of holding my hand when things felt tough, the way we'd look at each other across a room and silently communicate—it was in those moments that I found true peace. Now that he's gone, no vacation, no social event, no new purchase could bring that same comfort.

I remember trying to follow all the advice people gave me. "Take a vacation, you need to get away!" a friend said one day. So, I went. But sitting on a beach, looking at the ocean, I realized I couldn't feel the joy I used to. The waves were beautiful, but it was as if I was watching life from a distance, detached. "Why am I not enjoying this?" I thought. "What's wrong with me?"

Another time, I went to a restaurant with friends. "Let's order your favorite—pasta!" one of them joked. And as we sat there, laughing, I realized the food didn't taste the same anymore. My favorite delicacies—those things I used to savor—felt dull, like I was eating just to eat, not to enjoy. I smiled and nodded, pretending it was fine, but inside, I felt a little more empty.

One evening, I was talking to my friend. "I see you trying to be strong, Pankhuri," he said gently. "But are you really okay? You don't have to keep pretending to be happy." I didn't have an answer for her. I wanted to believe that the success, the career, the moments with my son, could somehow make everything right. But they didn't. It wasn't just the pain of missing Shivam—it was the deep, gnawing realization that I had handed my happiness over to him, and now, without him, I was lost.

I watched people who seemed to have it all together. Their homes were peaceful, their relationships steady. They had their challenges, but there was a quiet joy in their lives. I looked at them and thought, What do they have that I don't?

And then there was my son. He was a source of joy, without a doubt. His laughter, his tiny hands holding mine—those moments brought light to my life. But at the same time, there was always a quiet sadness that lingered. I couldn't help but mourn for Shivam, wishing he could be here to see our child grow. That mix of joy and sorrow made it hard for me to fully embrace happiness.

It took me a while to realize the truth—that I had placed my happiness in someone else's hands. Shivam had been my anchor, and when he was gone, I found myself adrift. But the reality is, happiness isn't something we find in someone else. I had forgotten that before Shivam, I was able to find joy in the simple things—laughter with friends, solo trips, quiet moments with myself. But I had handed over that power to him.

I see now that true happiness doesn't come from external sources. It's an internal power that we nurture within ourselves. The key is not in what we own or who we love—it's in learning to love ourselves, to embrace our own strength, and to find joy in just being. Happiness isn't something we chase; it's something we cultivate from within. And when we do that, no matter what life throws our way, we'll have the strength to face it.

One day, as I sat alone after putting my son to bed, a thought struck me. "If I can't find happiness in my own company, how can I ever feel fulfilled, no matter what else life gives me?" That question became the spark for a journey inward—a journey to discover the happiness I had forgotten how to nurture within myself.

I began small. I started journaling, writing down three things I was grateful for every night before bed. At first, it felt mechanical. "The house didn't fall apart today," I'd write sarcastically, or "The coffee was good." But over time, I noticed that these small moments of gratitude began to shift my perspective. Instead of focusing on what was missing, I started to see what was already there.

Meditation became another powerful tool. I remember sitting in my balcony one morning, listening to the sounds of the world waking up outside on road. It wasn't about silencing my thoughts—that's impossible. Instead, it was about sitting with them, letting them flow, and realizing that I didn't have to hold onto every single one.

Slowly, I began to reconnect with the things that brought me joy *before* Shivam. I started reading books that made me lose track of time, listening to music in my car when driving alone, and even taking my son to lunches and dinners. Each of these moments reminded me that happiness wasn't something I had to chase—it was something I could create.

As I continue this journey, I remember those words Shivam said: "Does it feel enough?" Maybe, in the end, the answer lies in knowing that the search for happiness is a lifelong one, but the real treasure is learning to find it in ourselves, right where we are.

The Lesson Learned

The greatest lesson I've learned in my 30 years is this: Happiness is not a destination; it's a way of being. It's a series of choices we make every day—choosing to appreciate what we have, choosing to nurture our inner selves, and choosing to find beauty in the smallest moments. It's not dependent on someone else, nor is it guaranteed by success or possessions. It's a practice, and like any practice, it requires patience and persistence.

Rebuilding happiness from within isn't about erasing grief or pretending life is perfect. It's about learning to coexist with life's messiness while creating moments of peace and joy. For me, it's a process I'm still learning, one day at a time. And while the pain of losing Shivam will always be a part of me, I've realized that I owe it to myself—and to him—to find my own light. Because happiness isn't something life hands you. It's something you grow, moment by moment, from the seeds you plant within your own heart.

A Simple Exercise for Reflection

If you, too, are searching for happiness, here's an exercise I've found transformative:

1. **Set aside 15 minutes.** Find a quiet spot where you can sit with your thoughts without interruptions.

2. **Take three deep breaths.** Feel the air fill your lungs and notice the sensation of your body grounding you.

3. **Ask yourself: What truly makes me feel alive?** Write down whatever comes to mind, no matter how small or insignificant it seems.

4. **Identify one action you can take today.** Maybe it's watching a sunset, calling an old friend, or simply enjoying a cup of tea without distractions.

5. **End with gratitude.** Write down three things you're thankful for in this moment. They can be as simple as, "I have a roof over my head," or as personal as, "I got through today."

Lesson 22

To Be Heard Without Judgment

As a child, my decision to become a psychologist wasn't born out of a grand dream or deep research. It wasn't inspired by an idol or a mentor. Instead, it was a decision rooted in an unmet need—a longing to become the person I wished I had in my life. I didn't dream of solving the mysteries of the human mind or uncovering groundbreaking psychological theories. I simply wanted to be someone who could truly listen, someone who could hear the pain hidden behind words and see the person behind the behavior.

You could say I was looking for someone to understand me. Growing up, I often felt judged rather than heard, misunderstood rather than supported. My anger wasn't rebellion—it was hurt. My aggression wasn't defiance—it was rejection. And my silence wasn't indifference—it was loneliness. But to those around me, I was simply labeled "difficult."

Even today, this longing to be understood lingers. Whenever I share my inner struggles, I'm met with advice, opinions, or judgment. Rarely does anyone simply listen. And while their intentions might be kind, their words don't lighten the burden—they only make it heavier.

We're often taught, through religious texts, movies, and societal ideals, that parents are always right, always have your best interests at heart, and therefore, must never be questioned. I agree—parents do want the best for their children. But what happens when their actions, however well-intentioned, only break you, leaving you weaker and lonelier?

In my experience, love wasn't the issue. My parents' love was undeniable, but their words and actions often felt like a constant stream of criticism. **"You're too sensitive," "You're picking fights over nothing," "You're the reason others are upset,"** or worse, **"Even your child's mental health will suffer because of you."**

These weren't one-off comments; they were recurring refrains that shaped how I saw myself. They instilled a sense of self-doubt so deep that I began questioning everything I did. Even as an adult, I found myself constantly trying to tick off the "good daughter" checklist:

- Complete education with flying colors.
- Marry at the right age.
- Prioritize family and responsibilities.
- Be polite, soft-spoken, and composed.
- Maintain relationships with relatives, no matter how toxic they were.

And yet, despite my efforts, I was still not enough. My decisions, whether to balance career and motherhood or to distance myself from unhealthy relationships, were seen as flaws.

Amidst this struggle, Shivam was my anchor. He didn't just love me; he valued me. He was the one person who didn't try to fix me or critique me. Instead, he simply stood by my side, offering unwavering support.

People sometimes ask me why I haven't moved on from losing him. They look at the imperfections in our relationship and ask, **"Don't you think what he did for you was just the bare minimum?"**

But to me, it was everything. Shivam didn't need to move mountains to prove his love. His presence, his understanding, and his acceptance were all I ever wanted. When I doubted myself, he reassured me. When I faltered, he held my hand. And when the world felt like it was closing in on me, he reminded me that I wasn't alone.

Unfortunately, fate had other plans. Losing him wasn't just the loss of a partner; it was the loss of my safe space. Shivam's love wasn't about grand gestures—it was about the quiet strength of his presence. And while others may call it "bare minimum," for me, it was everything.

People often say, "Be grateful for what you have," or, "Don't dwell on the past." I understand their intentions, but gratitude doesn't erase the scars of years spent feeling inadequate. Sometimes, all I wanted was for someone to say:

"It's okay if you couldn't handle certain relationships. We know it's hard."

"It's okay to cut ties with people who hurt you. Your peace matters more than their opinions."

These simple words could have healed so much. But instead, I was met with reminders to be grateful:

"Be thankful they let you live in their home."

"They're helping you raise your son."

"They're doing this out of love."

While I appreciated their support, gratitude didn't erase the pain of feeling misunderstood.

This emotional weight has followed me into every relationship I've had, even after becoming a mother. At night, when the world sleeps, I lie awake, grappling with questions that haunt me:

Why am I not good enough?

Why can't I ever seem to do the right thing?

Am I unlovable?

Was Shivam's love real, or did I burden him too?

Is my loneliness my punishment for not being enough?

My experiences didn't just shape my pain; they shaped my purpose. I became a psychologist because I wanted to offer others what I longed for: a space to be heard without judgment.

I wanted to tell children, "Your feelings are valid."

I wanted to tell adults, "You don't need to be perfect to be loved."

In helping others find their voice, I've started to rediscover my own. I'm learning to let go of the guilt and to accept that love and hurt can coexist.

This chapter isn't about blaming my parents or painting them as villains. I love them deeply, and I know they love me. But love doesn't erase pain. Healing begins when we acknowledge it, and sometimes, that starts with hearing the words we never got to hear.

The Lesson

Life has taught me that love and understanding are not mutually exclusive. It's possible to love someone deeply while also acknowledging the hurt they've caused. Healing doesn't come from pretending everything is fine or bottling up the pain; it comes from allowing ourselves to feel, to voice, and to validate our emotions.

A Simple Exercise for Reflection

To start your journey of healing and self-discovery, try this exercise:

Find a Quiet Space: Choose a time and place where you won't be disturbed for at least 30 minutes.

- Write a Letter to Someone Who Hurt You:

  Begin with, "Dear [Name], this is what I wish I could have said to you..."

- Pour your heart out. Write about how their words or actions made you feel, what you needed from them, and what you wish they could understand. Don't worry about structure or grammar—just let your thoughts flow.
- Reflect on Your Needs: After finishing the letter, take a moment to identify what you needed but didn't receive. Write those needs down as affirmations. For example:

  "I deserve to be heard without judgment."

  "My feelings are valid, even if others don't understand them."

- Release or Preserve: You don't have to share this letter with anyone. You can choose to keep it as a reminder of your growth or destroy it as a symbolic act of releasing the pain.

Lesson 23

Psychology – A Boon or a Burden?

When I first ventured into the world of psychology, I envisioned it as a superpower—a gift to understand, empathize, and heal. But life has a way of shattering even the most romanticized notions, and I found myself questioning whether this "gift" was a blessing or a curse. Sometimes, understanding others doesn't bring peace; it brings pain. Pain that you must endure quietly because you can see too much and feel too deeply.

This realization hit me hardest during the darkest chapter of my life—the day Shivam, my husband, left this world. With him, he took not just my dreams, but a sense of normalcy I would never regain. Yet, while I was grieving the love of my life and the father of my son, Cheeku, I found myself at the center of a storm of human behavior I never anticipated.

Grieving Shivam was one battle, but dealing with the world around me was another. In my rawest moments, I saw people's true faces—some concerned, some indifferent, some shockingly self-serving. Some were concerned about Shivam's belongings—his clothes, his gadgets, even the trivial things he left behind. Others, though well-meaning in their way, had their own agendas. There were whispers, quiet speculations about what would happen next. With whom would Cheeku live? What would become of me?

My in-laws, in their grief and perhaps an attempt to ensure Cheeku's future, suggested that I remarry. The plan? My brother-in-law and sister-in-law would adopt Cheeku, and I could "start fresh." While I know their intentions came from a place of love and concern, their words left me shattered. Was this really the time for such decisions? Couldn't my pain be acknowledged before solutions were forced upon me? I felt as though I was being pushed to trade my heartbreak for practicality, my son's future for my own healing. To this day, I wonder—why didn't my pain matter in that moment? Why couldn't I be allowed to grieve without the weight of their plans for my life?

And then, there were others. Relatives, acquaintances, people who revealed their true colors. I remember someone asking about a loan Shivam had taken, as if that was their biggest concern in the wake of his death. Another asked about a small piece of jewelry I had borrowed long ago, as though reclaiming it was their way of gaining control in the midst of chaos. I wanted to scream, to lash out, to tell them that I couldn't care less about their trinkets and debts when my world had crumbled. But psychology has a way of silencing your anger. It makes you pause, notice the tremble in their hands, the hesitation in their voices, the fear behind their actions. It made me realize they weren't being malicious—they were just lost in their own grief, unable to cope with the enormity of what had happened.

Still, understanding didn't make it easier. In fact, it made it worse. The more I empathized, the less I could fight back. My emotions became a battleground of anger and compassion. I wanted to confront them, but the part of me that understood their motives held me back. Empathy shackled me in ways I never anticipated.

And it wasn't just this time. I remember a close bond I had formed with someone—a woman I had always wished the best for, even when decisions in my favor could have gone against her. Despite my goodwill, there came a day when she accused me of betrayal, blaming me for things I had never even considered. Her words stung more than I can describe. I wanted to defend myself, to tell her how wrong she was. But then came that all-too-familiar pull of psychology, urging me to look deeper. I saw her pain, her struggle, and I realized she was as much a victim of her circumstances as I was of her accusations. I forgave her, not because she deserved it, but because I couldn't carry the weight of resentment.

Even though now we both talk again and share a cordial relationship, even the concern for each other, people around us often wonder—after everything that happened, how can we still be normal with each other? Honestly, we don't quite understand it ourselves. But what I suppose is that since she, too, is spiritual, we both carry somewhere the gift of forgiveness and the ability to see the soul beyond its actions. In fact, I too wonder—did I truly forgive, or did I just silence my pain under the weight of understanding? Psychology tells me she, too, suffered. But what about me? Did my healing get lost in my attempt to see her side?

I am sure she, too, carries bitter memories of that time, but the knowledge of psychology and spirituality sometimes blurs the lines—making me question whether such understanding is a gift or a burden.

But forgiveness doesn't erase the scars. It leaves you in a state of limbo, questioning whether you should let someone back into your life or walk away for good. It's a delicate balance—choosing between self-respect and understanding, dignity and reconciliation. With her, I chose to make peace, to maintain the bond while keeping my distance. Yet the discomfort lingered. Did I do the right thing? Or did I betray myself in the process?

This duality of psychology—its ability to grant both clarity and conflict—makes me question whether it's a boon or a burden. It allows me to see the "why" behind people's actions, but it also leaves me exposed to their raw, unfiltered truths. And sometimes, knowing too much only makes the pain harder to bear.

The Lesson

In the midst of these challenges, I've learned that understanding human behavior is not always liberating—it can be a weight you carry. Psychology teaches you to empathize, but it doesn't teach you how to shield yourself from the hurt. I've learned that while it's important to see others' pain, it's equally important to acknowledge your own. Sometimes, the kindest thing you can do for yourself is to let go—not just of the people who hurt you, but of the need to understand their reasons.

A Simple Exercise for Reflection

Here's an exercise that can help you navigate the complexities of human behavior:

Emotion Map: Draw a large circle and divide it into two halves. Label one half "What I Feel" and the other "What They Might Be Feeling."

1. In the first half, write down your raw emotions about a situation—anger, hurt, confusion.
2. In the second half, try to write down what the other person might have been experiencing. What fears, insecurities, or pain might have driven their actions?

Reflection: Step back and observe the map. Notice where your emotions and theirs overlap. Ask yourself:

1. Is there a way to address both sets of emotions without compromising your well-being?
2. What boundaries can you set to protect your peace?

Lesson 24

Grief is a Personal Journey

Grief has a way of stripping life of its colors, leaving behind only shades of gray. But what many fail to grasp is that no two people grieve the same way. It's deeply personal, shaped by the role someone played in your life. It cannot be compared—not between two widows of the same age, not even between family members grieving the same loss.

When I lost Shivam, my world came crashing down. He wasn't just my husband; he was my anchor, my partner in every sense of the word. Losing him didn't just leave an absence in my life—it shattered my past, my present, and my future.

But within just three months, people began expecting me to "move on." It was as if there was a silent, unspoken deadline for grief, after which life was supposed to return to normal. There were constant suggestions and expectations:

They said, 'You should think about Cheeku. He needs a father.' But did they think about me? About how I was supposed to mother him while my heart was still shattered? They told me others had 'moved on,' as if grief had a road-map that I had failed to follow. But how do you move on from losing the person who was the very fabric of your existence?

I knew most of these words came from a place of care, but that didn't make them hurt any less. Each suggestion stung like salt on an open wound. I vividly remember when my in-laws suggested I consider remarriage. They even offered a plan: my sister-in-law and brother-in-law could adopt Cheeku, and I could start a new life. I could see their pain and the best of their intentions, but I couldn't understand how they didn't see the impossibility of what they were asking. Did my pain not matter? Did they think I could ever leave my son or that someone could ever replace Shivam?

One night, sitting in my room—which was now my sister-in-law's room—I held Cheeku close. As I looked at his innocent face, I whispered through my tears, "They don't understand, do they? They don't understand that we've lost everything."

Even participating in normal life events felt impossible. When there was a family wedding just a few months later, I chose not to attend. I knew my presence would bring a heaviness to the celebrations, and I couldn't bear the thought of being there without Shivam. How could I sit through rituals that reminded me of everything I had lost?

Festivals became equally unbearable. The first Diwali without Shivam was excruciating. The house was lit with diyas, but the light only magnified the darkness within me. Rituals that once brought joy felt like cruel reminders of his absence. I stayed in my room, pretending to rest, while everyone else tried to carry on as usual.

People compared my grief to others'. They'd point out women who remarried soon after losing their husbands, saying, "Look, she moved on. That's how life works." What they didn't understand was that for them, Shivam was a cherished memory, someone they missed during a festival or a casual conversation. For me, he was everything—my past, my present, and the future I had envisioned.

It took me three years to gather the courage to fully participate in a wedding. That moment came when my brother, Prakhar, was getting married. The day before the wedding, I cried relentlessly, mourning Shivam's absence, knowing how much he would have helped Prakhar at every step as the perfect brother-in-law.

On the wedding day, I resolved to push my grief aside. I wanted to see Prakhar happy, and I didn't want my tears to mark his celebrations. I engrossed myself in the music and dance, distracting myself from the pain.

But just before the baraat, as Prakhar climbed onto the horse, my composure broke. Shivam's brother stood in his place, performing the duties Shivam would have done. The weight of that realization overwhelmed me, and I found myself crying uncontrollably. My sisters quickly pulled me aside, shielding me from view so that Prakhar or anyone else wouldn't notice.

The event manager, who had been watching from a distance, came up to me. Consoling me in a calm but firm voice, she said, "This is the time for your baraat performance. Would you like to miss this opportunity? This moment will never come back." Her words jolted me back to reality.

As the horse and the baraat approached the main gate, I wiped my tears, took a deep breath, and joined the celebration. I danced with all the energy I could muster, smiling through the pain, ensuring that no one saw the storm raging inside me. For those few hours, I became the sister who only wanted her brother's happiness, and not a soul realized how much I was hurting.

Some people heal by surrounding themselves with others, some by embracing solitude. For me, it was a mix of both—a wedding that forced me to confront my loss and a solo trip that let me breathe through it. My grief didn't fit into society's template, and I finally realized—it never had to. Shivam is not coming back. My family is now of two—me and Cheeku.

Everyday events still feel like mountains to climb, but I've learned to gather myself up, time and again. My tears have become habitual—they well up in my eyes but rarely roll down.

The Lesson

Grief is not a formula, nor is it a journey others can map out for you. Some wounds heal, some remain, and some transform into a quiet strength. The world may not always understand your grief—but that's okay. Because in the end, only you can define what healing looks like for you and even in moments of unbearable pain, you can find strength. It's not about pretending the pain doesn't exist—it's about choosing to live in spite of it.

A Simple Exercise for Reflection

Take a moment to reflect on the events or situations that have tested your emotional resilience. Write down one instance where you pulled yourself together despite overwhelming pain. What did you learn about yourself in that moment? How can you apply that strength to other areas of your life?

Lesson 25

Acceptance—The Struggle Within

Acceptance often sounds peaceful, like finding a calm harbor in a storm. But honestly, it's anything but serene. It's a messy, raw, and constant battle that tests every ounce of your being. It forces you to face the unthinkable, to navigate chaos when every part of you screams to hold on.

For the longest time, I thought acceptance meant surrendering, giving up. It felt like admitting defeat, like moving forward meant leaving behind everything and everyone I loved. My head knew I couldn't change what happened, but my heart stubbornly clung to the past.

Morena… just the name makes my stomach churn. It's a small town in Madhya Pradesh, and it's where my world shattered. It's where I lost Shivam in a terrible accident. For everyone else, it's just another place on the map. For me, it's a landscape haunted by grief. Every street corner whispers his absence, making the ache even worse. Even thinking about going back there feels like ripping open a wound that never fully healed.

I remember one visit so clearly. I was alone in a dimly lit room, holding Shivam's picture. His eyes, usually so full of life, just stared back at me, reflecting the huge emptiness he left behind. The longer I looked, the heavier it got. The walls felt like they were closing in, memories of what could have been crashing into the harsh reality of what *was*. Grief hit me in waves, so strong I could barely breathe. I had to face all the emotions I'd tried to bury. I tried everything – pills, meditation, therapy – but nothing touched the pain. Every other day, I'd be sobbing into my pillow, clutching Shivam's photo, begging him to see how much I was hurting. "Why did you betray me? Why did you leave me like this?" I'd scream into the darkness. "How am I supposed to live without you? I've forgotten how to live without you!" I'd beg him to come back, apologizing a million times. "I'm so sorry! Did I expect too much? Was I so awful that leaving was the only peace you could find?" It went on like that until one day… it just clicked. He *wasn't* coming back. He *wouldn't* be coming back. Even saying it to myself felt impossible. "I'm a widow," I'd whisper, practicing the words whenever someone asked about my marital status. I wouldn't lie, but those words… they felt like lead in my mouth. But I accepted it. He was gone. And that's when things started to shift, just a little.

Then there's Cheeku. He's my anchor, my biggest joy, but he's also a constant reminder of what's missing. Watching other dads with their kids, laughing and playing… it's like rubbing salt in the wound. Cheeku doesn't say much, but I see it in his eyes. The unspoken questions, the quiet strength… it's like looking in a mirror. I try so hard to be everything he needs, but the guilt… the guilt of not giving him a complete family… it's crushing.

And then there's me. I miss having someone, someone to share life with, the good and the bad. Seeing couples together, happy and comfortable, it can be both nice and incredibly painful. Sometimes, the loneliness is overwhelming. But I'm starting to understand that this is my path, for now at least. Maybe companionship isn't in the cards for me right now. So, instead of waiting for someone to fill the emptiness, I'm learning to be my own rock. It's not ideal, but it's making me stronger in ways I never imagined.

Mom always says, "Crying over what's gone won't bring it back. Focus on what you have and deal with it." She means well, and I know she's right. But every little setback, every new challenge... it just wears me down. Some days, I feel like I'm losing hope, stuck in this endless loop of pain, exhaustion, and despair. And the physical stuff... nobody talks about that part. I didn't get any time to recover after having Cheeku, and my body is paying the price. I get these weird aches and pains, I'm always tired, and sometimes I have panic attacks. It's like my body is screaming, "Slow down! Heal!" But life just keeps pushing me forward. Acceptance wasn't some big "aha!" moment. It was a gradual process, a million tiny moments of surrender. The toughest part was accepting that Shivam was gone forever, that no amount of tears or anger could change anything. Each step towards acceptance felt like peeling off a layer of skin, exposing wounds I wasn't ready to see. But with each layer, I found glimpses of peace, a quiet voice whispering, "You can do this."

And it's still not easy. Grief still comes back, sharp and strong, like no time has passed. But I'm learning to carry it differently. It doesn't define me anymore. It's just... there. Like a shadow. And instead of letting it drag me down, I'm choosing to let it remind me of the love we shared.

The Lesson

Acceptance isn't about erasing pain or forgetting the past. It's about making peace with the uncontrollable, finding resilience in the face of loss, and embracing life despite its imperfections. True acceptance lies in coexisting with grief, finding joy amidst sorrow, and building a future even when the foundation feels cracked. It's about choosing yourself every day, even when the world feels overwhelming.

Self-Reflection Exercise

- **Identify the Pain Points:** Reflect on three areas of your life where acceptance feels difficult. Write them down, describing why they feel challenging.
- **Acknowledge Your Emotions:** Take a moment to sit with your feelings. Write about the emotions these challenges stir within you—fear, anger, sadness, or even hope.
- **Visualize the First Step:** For each pain point, consider one small action you can take toward acceptance. It could be a conversation, a mindset shift, or a simple daily habit.

Lesson 26

Counseling – A Journey to Meet Myself and Help Myself

When I chose to become a counselor, it wasn't simply about acquiring knowledge or adding a title to my name. It was something far deeper. At the time, I didn't fully understand why this path called to me so strongly. It felt like a compass pointing me toward something significant, something I couldn't articulate yet. Looking back now, I realize that counseling wasn't just about helping others—it was also about helping myself.

The real depth of my decision didn't hit me until I started practicing, especially during my internship. Sitting across from clients, listening to their stories, something unexpected began to happen. Their words started resonating in ways I hadn't anticipated. It wasn't just empathy or professional concern—I was meeting fragments of myself in their experiences, as if their pain and struggles were reflecting my own.

Before I even began this journey, I faced skepticism—not from within, but from others. When I was about to join an initiative related to counseling, some people hesitated. They weren't sure if I was ready. "Are you sure you'll be able to handle emotional cases?" they asked, concerned that my past experiences might make me overly empathetic or vulnerable. They worried that I might crumble under the weight of someone else's trauma.

At first, their doubts stung. I knew I had been through a lot—trauma, heartbreak, emotional battles—but instead of weakening me, those experiences had forged resilience. They had taught me lessons that books and lectures never could. The truth was, my past had shaped me into someone who could connect with others on a deeper level. It wasn't a burden; it was a gift.

One of my most memorable cases was a ninth-grade girl. She came to me not for therapy, but for career guidance. At first, our conversations revolved around goals, ambitions, and the ever-looming question, "What do you want to be when you grow up?" She was bright—her academic performance reflected her intelligence—but there was something beneath her confident exterior that she hadn't yet put into words.

As our sessions progressed, she began to open up. "I feel so lost," she admitted one day, her voice faltering. "All my friends know what they want to do. They're so clear about their goals, their dreams… but me? I feel like I'm just floating. I don't want to disappoint my parents, but I don't even know what I want."

Her words hit me like a wave. I had been that girl once—caught between the expectations of others and the confusion within myself. She also shared something more personal, something I hadn't expected. "I feel like my mom loves my siblings more than me," she said quietly. "She's so much kinder to them. With me, it's just criticism after criticism. No matter how hard I try, I'm never enough."

Hearing her say those words felt like déjà vu. It was as if she was giving voice to emotions I had carried for years. Growing up, I, too, had felt the sting of being misunderstood, of being held to a higher standard than those around me. I had internalized it as unfairness, even rejection.

But as a counselor, I had to maintain my professional boundaries. I couldn't let my personal experiences cloud the process. Instead, I focused on guiding her toward reframing her perceptions. I helped her explore the possibility that her mother's strictness wasn't born out of favoritism but rather out of belief in her potential.

And as I spoke those words to her, something shifted in me, too. I realized that maybe—just maybe—my own parents had been doing the same. Maybe their expectations and criticisms weren't meant to hurt me but to push me to be the best version of myself. For the first time, I began to let go of the resentment I had carried for so long.

Another case that deeply moved me was a young woman who came to me seeking counselling. She wanted someone to guide her; she needed a space to unburden herself.

Her story unfolded slowly, each session revealing a little more. She had grown up as the child of a single parent, shouldering responsibilities far beyond her years. "I've never felt like a child," she admitted one day. "While other kids were playing, I was worrying about bills or making sure my parent was okay. I've always had to be the strong one."

Her words were heavy, yet they carried a quiet strength. But beneath that strength was an ache—a longing to be seen, to be heard, to feel, even for a moment, like she didn't have to carry the weight of the world on her shoulders.

She did ask for counseling but due to the professional limitations of the college where I was teaching, I couldn't offer her therapy. So instead, she asked me to guide her as a life coach.

"I don't trust anyone else," she said earnestly. "If you can't counsel me, at least help me figure out how to navigate this."

I couldn't say no. Life coaching wasn't the same as therapy, but it was something I could do within the boundaries of my role. And because this was something I felt deeply about, I refused to charge her any fees. This wasn't about professional obligations; it was about helping someone who reminded me so much of myself.

As we worked together, she shared how lonely she felt, how the weight of responsibility had made her grow up too fast. She spoke about never knowing the luxury of being carefree, of feeling like her own dreams were always secondary to her obligations.

Her story was painfully familiar. In helping her navigate her challenges, I found myself reflecting on my own. I encouraged her to create small moments of joy for herself, to remember that even amidst responsibilities, she deserved to dream, to laugh, to feel alive. And as I said those words to her, I realized they were words I needed to hear, too.

The Lesson

Counseling has taught me that life has a way of weaving our pain into our purpose. Every struggle, every heartbreak, and every moment of confusion I've faced has prepared me for this work. It has given me the empathy to connect with others, not from a place of pity but from a place of shared humanity.

In helping others, I've found pieces of myself. I've learned that healing isn't a linear journey—it's a cycle of giving and receiving, of breaking and rebuilding. Each session, each client, each story has been a step closer to understanding myself and my place in this world.

Sometimes, the best way to heal is to help.

A Simple Exercise for Reflection

For one week, focus on truly listening when someone shares their story with you. Resist the urge to judge or offer solutions immediately. Instead, reflect on their words and how they resonate with your own experiences. Notice how this practice deepens your understanding and connection.

Lesson 27

The Blame Game

For most of my life, I carried a heavy weight—blame. I blamed my parents for almost everything that didn't go right in my life. And I didn't hold back, even in this book. One of my biggest accusations against them was that their decisions had derailed my dreams.

I blamed my father for not letting me pursue psychology right after 12th grade. I told him countless times that because of his decision, I got stuck in BBA and MBA—fields I had no passion for. I felt like he had forced me into a life I never wanted.

I blamed them for not letting me study outside Indore, for keeping me sheltered and limiting my exposure to opportunities. I told myself that because of them, I couldn't grow, couldn't spread my wings. I blamed them for pressuring me into marrying early when I had dreams of studying abroad. "If you want to marry Shivam," they had said, "then you have to marry now."

Every time I saw someone else living my dream, I felt a pang of jealousy. And when my parents appreciated others for achieving the things I wanted for myself, it stung even more. I thought to myself, They never gave me the chance, but they applaud others for doing what I could have done.

Even today, my father doesn't like that I leave for work early in the morning. He still says, "Don't focus on earning or money. Just do something for the sake of time pass or as a hobby." I used to feel hurt by those words. Did he not see me as capable? Did they not expect anything of me beyond marriage and family?

For years, I lived in this narrative of blame. It was my comfort zone, my explanation for every failure and missed opportunity. But lately, something has shifted in me. A slow but profound change in perspective began to take shape.

The first crack in my wall of blame appeared during an argument with my father. It was one of those heated discussions where words fly out unchecked, raw and cutting. I had said to him, "Because of you, I'm a failure."

His face fell, but being as hot-tempered as I am, he didn't stay silent for long. His voice rose as he retorted, "So, am I the only one responsible for all your failures?"

"Yes, of course!" I shot back. "Who else? You never gave me opportunities. I always had to obey you."

What he said next shook me to my core.

"No, I am not the reason. *You* are," he said firmly. "If you had the capability, the confidence in yourself, and the passion for your goals, you wouldn't have given up so easily. You would have fought for what you wanted. You would have become stubborn, snatched the opportunities, and run after your dreams if they mattered to you so much—just like Shivam did.

"In front of him, you never gave up. Even when challenges came your way—when your engagement and marriage were postponed due to unforeseen events, when situations arose that would've made anyone else walk away—you held on. You strengthened your determination to marry Shivam. If you could fight for that, why couldn't you fight for your dreams?"

I was stunned into silence. His words hit me like a wave, drowning my excuses and leaving me gasping for clarity. I wanted to argue back, but I couldn't. Deep down, I knew he was right.

I cried that day—not because of his words but because of the truth they uncovered. I had never fought for my dreams the way I had fought for other things in my life. That fire, that relentless zeal, had been missing.

That moment became a turning point for me. I realized that life would always test me by presenting two-way paths. Each time, it would be up to me to choose the one that led to my goals. And if I wanted something badly enough, I had to be willing to fight for it, no matter who or what stood in my way.

My father's words replayed in my mind over and over: "If your dreams mattered to you, you wouldn't have given up."

I had spent so much time blaming others—especially my parents—for the choices I hadn't made, for the opportunities I hadn't seized. But the truth was, the blame lay with me. I had let fear, comfort, and compliance dictate my path.

Yet, as I've grown older, I've also started to see my father's perspective more clearly. When I hear him say now, even at 30, "Don't work so hard. Don't worry about earning money for Cheeku," I no longer feel dismissed. I understand that it's not because he doesn't see potential in me. It's because his love for me has always been so deep that he, like my grandfather, never wanted me to suffer or struggle.

I won't say that he was right to shield me from struggles—because I've learned that growth often comes from hardship—but I now recognize that his intentions were never wrong. He still assures me that I don't need to worry about my future, that he will make all the necessary arrangements for Cheeku and me. And when he transfers large sums of money into my account without warning, it's his way of saying, *You're not alone.*

But what he doesn't understand is that I've lost the capacity to rely on anyone after losing Shivam. All my dreams, my expectations, my future were tied to Shivam, and his absence took it all away. I had placed my entire identity in him, and when he left, I was left with nothing but myself.

That's why now, I can't bring myself to depend on anyone—not even my father. I don't want to be someone else's responsibility. I want to rely on myself, to build my own identity, to stand on my own two feet. My independence is not just a desire; it's a necessity born from the ashes of my loss.

The Lesson

Blaming others is easy. It's comfortable, even satisfying in a way. But it keeps you stuck. It wasn't until I stopped blaming my parents and took accountability for my own choices that I began to grow.

The lesson I've learned in 30 years is this: if you want something badly enough, you have to fight for it. You can't wait for permission or approval. You can't blame others when things don't go your way. Your life is your responsibility.

And while I've learned to forgive my parents and understand their intentions, I've also learned that my path forward lies in self-reliance. I am determined to create a life that is truly mine—defined by my choices, my struggles, and my triumphs. This, I believe, is the ultimate act of love—for myself and for the ones who have always wanted the best for me.

A Simple Exercise for Reflection

Step 1: Identify Your Blame Patterns

- Write down three situations in your life where you have blamed others for your struggles or missed opportunities.
- Who did you blame? Why?

Step 2: Analyze Your Role

- For each situation, ask yourself:
    - Could I have done something differently?
    - What actions or inactions contributed to the outcome?
    - If I had fought harder for what I wanted, how might things have been different?

Step 3: Shift to Ownership

- Rewrite each situation by replacing blame with accountability.
- Example: Instead of "My parents didn't allow me to study what I wanted," reframe it as "I didn't assert myself strongly enough to pursue my passion."
- How does this shift in perspective make you feel?

Step 4: Plan Your Next Steps

- Pick one area of your life where you still feel stuck due to blame.
- What steps can you take today to reclaim control over that aspect?

- How will you ensure that you take responsibility for your future choices?

Step 5: Daily Affirmation

- Write a statement that reinforces your commitment to self-accountability. Example:
    - "I am responsible for my life. I choose to take ownership of my decisions and create the future I desire."

Lesson 28

The Complexity of Love and Relationships

Life has a strange way of showing us the shades of people—their kindness, their flaws, their love, and their wounds, all tangled together. Throughout this book, I have spoken about moments where I felt deeply hurt—by my in-laws, by my own family, by friends who made me feel lonely, guilty, or even invisible. And yet, in the same breath, I have also shared moments where these very people stood beside me, holding me up when I could barely stand.

It is confusing, isn't it? To wonder whether the people in your life are good or bad. I, too, have struggled with this question. There are parts of me that can never forget the impatience, the insensitivity, the moments I felt ignored or less loved. But there are also parts of me that cannot overlook the hands that held me when I was falling. The same people who hurt me at times have also forgiven me when I wasn't at my best.

I remember, just two days after losing Shivam, I did something that shocked everyone—I asked my mother to switch on the TV.

A heavy silence followed. My mother hesitated, then whispered, *"No, this is not the right time. What will people think?"*

But before anyone could judge me, my mother-in-law stood firm. *"Switch on the TV,"* she said. *"If she wants it on, let her have it."*

And so, the TV was switched on. Every night, I would keep it playing until 2 or 3 AM, the flickering light breaking the suffocating darkness of my thoughts. My mother-in-law would lie on the bed beside it. My own mother worried she might be getting disturbed, but she never complained.

I often wondered where she found the strength. Even after losing her son, she chose to stand by me, taking care of my seemingly irrational demands. But I had my reasons.

Even though my room was full of people, it suddenly felt empty—because Shivam was not there. No longer did I hear his voice calling me every now and then—

"Pankhu, kya kar rahi hai?" (Pankhu, what are you doing?)

"Pankhu, sab vadiya?" (Pankhu, everything good?)

"Pankhu, main 10 minute doston se mil aau?" (Pankhu, can I go meet my friends for 10 minutes?)

"Pankhu betu, tujhe kuch khana hai? Kuch la du?" (Pankhu dear, do you want something to eat? Should I bring something for you?)

His absence was deafening. The room that once echoed with his presence now buzzed with people talking—some out of genuine concern, others throwing anxious questions about my future, making me even more restless. So, I turned on the TV—not to watch it, but to drown out the voices. The meaningless sound of the TV was more comforting than the reality around me.

It was my mother-in-law who understood my pain in ways no one else did. When others acted out of their own grief and insecurities, suggesting that Cheeku be taken away to lessen their sorrow, she was the one who assured me, *"I know the pain of losing a son, and I won't let that happen to you."*

When my own parents and in-laws suggested that I move back to Morena with Cheeku so that they could feel some comfort in having him around, she was the one who gathered strength and told me, *"If you live here, you won't be able to move forward. You need space, away from people's mindsets and their limitations."*

Sometimes, she would dream for me. She imagined that, one day, someone would fall in love with me again in the most filmy, grand way. That someone would enter my life and love me even more than Shivam did.

But my father-in-law was different. He wanted me to be happy, yet the thought of me and Cheeku moving away after I remarried unsettled him. He never said it outright, but I could sense his struggle. Still, with a heavy heart, he would tell me, *"Beta, look for someone and marry in time. We don't know how long we will be around to take care of both of you."*

Many times, he was the one who called me, his voice carrying the same unwavering assurance as my father's—*"Tujhe paiso ki ya kisi bhi cheez ki chinta karna hi kyu hai, jab main baitha hoon yaha?"* (Why should you worry about money or anything else when I am here?)

Once, I hesitated and told him, *"Paapaji, you too are going through a difficult time. I don't want to burden you."*

His reply was firm, almost scolding me for even thinking that way—*"So what? Is it your fault that we are going through a bad phase?"*

And then there was my brother-in-law—always just a call away. We had our share of disagreements, our moments of frustration, but no matter what, he never ignored my calls. Every time I reached out, he listened, helped—not just by sending money but by guiding me, finding ways to solve my problems, ensuring that I never felt alone.

My other brother-in-law, the quiet one, expressed his love in actions rather than words. Whenever we visited Morena, he would fulfill every little demand of Cheeku, unknowingly prioritizing him over his own children. I could see it in their eyes when they played with him or spoke to him—they, too, searched for Shivam in his laughter.

There are times, still, when my mother-in-law looks at me, and I see Shivam reflected in her gaze. She tells me that I am her Shivam now, and her voice trembles with a love that transcends loss. When she talks to me, it's as if she's reaching for him, bridging the impossible distance. Her anxieties about me, especially the weight of financial burdens I carry, echo the tender care she always gave him. In those moments, my heart swells with a mixture of love and grief, and I whisper to Shivam, "You were right. She is love itself." We've had our share of difficult moments, before and after he was gone, but our bond is deeper than in-law ties.

Shivam and I were talking about his family one day. "You know," he said, "my parents were actually expecting a girl before I came along. They were a little surprised, to say the least."

I chuckled. "So, you were supposed to be a princess?"

"Something like that," he replied, grinning. Then, his expression turned a little more serious. "He also said, 'Pankhu, be like a daughter to my mom, the daughter she always wanted.'"

I looked at him, my heart swelling with affection. "I will, Shivam. I promise."

After Shivam was gone, the pain was almost unbearable. There were times I wanted to shut everyone out, including his family. They unintentionally said hurtful things in their own grief. And I'm sure, in my own grief, I wasn't perfect either. It's human nature, isn't it? We often don't see our own part in things. But I can only speak to my experience. And what I felt was the need to honor Shivam's memory. So, I tried, with whatever capacity I had, to become the daughter they never had but always wanted.

I understand their pain. I understand that grief manifests in countless ways, that when faced with such a profound loss, we instinctively cling to what remains, protect what we have left. I may not fully comprehend their perspective, their specific experience of loss, but I understand grief. We were all trying to deal with this new, awful reality. We were all hurting, all trying to figure out how to live with this huge hole in our lives. And maybe that's why, even when we hurt each other or things got messed up, we always found our way back. Maybe because we are all connected by one thing—our love for Shivam and Cheeku.

The Lesson

Relationships are never perfect. The people we love will sometimes disappoint us, misunderstand us, or even unintentionally hurt us. But true love—whether in family, friendships, or partnerships—doesn't vanish because of flaws. It finds a way to hold on, to forgive, to evolve.

Love is not about perfection; it is about presence. It is about showing up, again and again, despite the pain, despite the past. I have learned that people are not entirely good or bad; they are just human—carrying their own struggles, insecurities, and limitations. And despite everything, love finds a way to persist.

A Simple Exercise for Reflection

Take a moment to reflect on your relationships—past and present. Answer the following questions in a journal or through quiet introspection:

1. **Identify a moment of hurt:** Recall a time when someone you loved disappointed or hurt you. How did that experience shape your perception of them?

2. **Recognize the love beneath the pain:** Have they also shown love, care, or support in ways that you may have overlooked?

3. **Explore your own role:** Have there been times when you may have hurt or disappointed someone unintentionally? How did they respond?

4. **Reframe the narrative:** Instead of seeing people as "good" or "bad," how can you understand them as complex individuals with strengths and weaknesses, just like you?

5. **Letting go or holding on:** Are there relationships that deserve healing? If so, what small step can you take toward forgiveness or understanding today?

Lesson 29

Superpowers of a Mother

When you become a mother, you unlock a reservoir of strength you never knew existed—a kind of superpower that seems straight out of a movie but is deeply rooted in reality. This power doesn't just emerge from love but also from an instinct to protect, nurture, and persevere, no matter how tough the situation gets. For me, this transformation wasn't immediate; it was forged through trials, fears, and the absence of the one person I thought I couldn't live without—Shivam.

Within thirteen days of Shivam's passing away, I faced a moment that still feels surreal when I look back. Our room had an uninvited guest—a lizard. We were quite used to its occasional appearances, but this one had the audacity to get on the bed sometimes, which terrified me to no end. Shivam always took care of it. Whether it was the middle of the night or during his busiest hour, he would calmly shoo it out, often laughing at my exaggerated reactions.

But this time, Shivam wasn't there.

I was sharing the room with my mother and mother-in-law. They were grieving too, utterly exhausted from days of emotional turmoil. When I pleaded with them to get rid of the lizard, they tried half-heartedly but gave up, assuring me it wouldn't harm anyone. "Just sleep; nothing will happen," they said.

But I couldn't. I wasn't scared for myself anymore—I was terrified for Cheeku. He was asleep on the bed, and all I could think about was the lizard crawling over him. My mind conjured endless worst-case scenarios.

I had just delivered Cheeku and still had stitches from the surgery. My body ached, and I could barely stand without support. But as I watched that lizard move around the room, something shifted inside me. I decided I couldn't take the risk of falling asleep, not when Cheeku might be in harm's way.

I picked him up, cradling his tiny body in my arms, and began pacing the room. For three to four hours, I walked from one corner to another, fighting the pain in my legs and the exhaustion in my soul. Every minute felt like an eternity, but I refused to sit down or let my guard down.

Even now, I wonder how I managed it that night. I didn't have the strength to stand for five minutes, let alone hours. But something bigger than me took over—a mother's willpower, fueled by nothing but love and the instinct to protect.

This moment was the first of many that taught me what it meant to be a mother without Shivam by my side. There was no one to lean on, no one to share the burden. But each time I was tested, I found a strength I never knew existed within me.

Then while I was pregnant, Shivam and I spent hours imagining the kind of parents we would become. Our discussions would oscillate between deep talks and light-hearted teasing.

He loved to joke that I would crumble under pressure. "When Cheeku comes home crying because a boy hit him, you'll cry even harder before consoling him!" he'd say, trying to get a rise out of me.

I'd retort sarcastically, "At least I won't be reckless like you—always too brave for your own good! I'll make sure our child is sensible and responsible."

Shivam would laugh and counter, "Don't worry; our baby will inherit my bravery, not your constant worrying!"

His words didn't bother me back then because I knew he'd be there. I could lean on him, trusting that he'd handle the tough situations while I took care of the rest. But life had other plans.

Cheeku was about 1.5 years old when one of the most terrifying nights of my life unfolded. I was teaching tuition classes while my mom looked after him. As she cleaned the kitchen, Cheeku's mischievous little self found a brush soaked in detergent and, like any curious toddler, put it in his mouth.

By the time I returned home, his stomach was upset, and he had started having frequent loose motions. My mom, scared of my reaction, downplayed the severity, hoping it would resolve on its own. But as the hours passed, his condition worsened. His cries of discomfort echoed in the house, and my panic grew.

It was 9 p.m. All nearby clinics were closed, and his pediatrician wasn't answering her phone. I felt paralyzed. My father wasn't home, and I didn't know where to go. In my panic, I grabbed Cheeku, took my nani along, and started driving aimlessly, searching for help.

After several failed attempts to find an open clinic, I called Yash, who managed to find a doctor in his neighborhood. I rushed there, tears welling up but refusing to fall. When the doctor suggested hospitalization, a wave of dread washed over me. Memories of a similar incident when Cheeku was just four months old haunted me—nights in Morena where I had watched him being pricked with needles for drips. Back then, Shivam's absence had felt unbearable; now, it was all on me.

I begged the doctor to try medication first and promised to take Cheeku to the hospital if it didn't work. Thankfully, the medicines helped, and Cheeku started recovering. That night, I stayed awake by his side, silently crying as I replayed the events in my mind. Despite the panic and fear, I had somehow managed to hold it all together.

Another time, Cheeku developed a fever that simply refused to come down. The medicines I had at home weren't helping, and his pediatrician wasn't available. I was told to wait until the morning, but the idea of waiting overnight with my baby in distress was unbearable. Every minute that passed felt like a ticking clock, and desperation consumed me.

I wrapped Cheeku in a blanket and drove out into the night. Clinic after clinic turned me away. Doctors were either unavailable or unwilling to see us without an appointment. By the third clinic, I was almost in tears, begging the receptionist to let us in.

Finally, a doctor agreed to help. As I sat in his office watching him examine Cheeku, relief flooded my entire being. Driving home that night, exhausted but calmer, I realized how far I had come. I wasn't the woman who needed someone else to handle the hard times anymore, though I wished to be. I had become someone who could rise to the occasion for the sake of her child.

These moments—and many others like them—taught me that motherhood doesn't allow you the luxury of staying weak. You don't get to sit on the sidelines, waiting for someone else to take charge. Every time life threw a challenge my way, I surprised myself with my own strength.

A Lesson

Motherhood doesn't just change you; it transforms you. It's not about being fearless but about pushing through the fear because your child's safety and happiness matter more than anything else. Strength isn't about having no limits; it's about discovering that your limits are far greater than you ever imagined.

You don't need a hero to save the day. Sometimes, you become the hero you never thought you could be.

A Simple Exercise for Reflection

1. Recall a moment when you had to step up despite being scared or unsure.
   - What gave you the courage to act?
   - How did that moment change your perception of your abilities?
2. Think about someone who used to be your source of strength.
   - How have they influenced your life?
   - How can you honor their memory or role by embodying their qualities?
3. Write down three ways you can tap into your inner strength during tough times.
   - What strategies can help you stay calm and focused under pressure?
   - How can you remind yourself of your past victories?

Lesson 30

Rising from Ashes – A Widow's Journey

As I pen down this final lesson, it feels like both a conclusion and a beginning—a bridge between the 30 years I've lived and the life that still lies ahead. If I'm granted another 30 years, I hope they are guided by the clarity and resilience this chapter has given me.

But this lesson isn't just about me; it's about every widow who finds herself thrust into a world that refuses to see her as whole, as capable, as enough.

From the day I lost Shivam, the world seemed to narrow down my existence to one recurring question: *"When will you remarry?"*

At first, I dismissed it, thinking it was well-meaning concern cloaked in societal expectations. But the frequency and insistence of the question began to wear me down. No matter what I did or said, people circled back to the same script:

- Asking, "Are you planning to remarry?"
- Advising, "You should marry soon—for Cheeku's sake."
- Criticizing, "Your stubbornness is hurting your son's future."

When challenges arise, the comments become sharper:

"This is why we told you to remarry earlier—look at the consequences now."

"All you need to do is marry, and your life and Cheeku's life will improve."

I've heard these statements so often they've become a script I could recite in my sleep.

Widows are burdened with an impossible task: to grieve quietly, rebuild quickly, and fit neatly into the expectations of a world that cannot handle their independence. The world offers one-size-fits-all solutions as if remarriage is a magical cure for grief, struggle, and the sleepless nights of single parenthood.

No one asks, *"Are you strong enough to stand on your own now?"*

"Are you independent now?"

No one offers, *"How can we help you rebuild your life?"*

"How can we help make your space safer and more supportive?"

Instead, the focus was always on what I supposedly lacked: a man, a partner, a societal stamp of approval. Rarely was I seen as enough—strong, capable, and whole on my own.

For the first two and a half years, the very thought of remarriage felt impossible, even offensive. My heart, broken and bleeding, couldn't fathom the idea of opening itself to someone else. I wasn't ready—not emotionally, spiritually, or practically. I was still navigating a labyrinth of grief, still trying to find my footing in a world that felt so unfamiliar without Shivam.

Every time someone brought up remarriage, it felt like a betrayal of the love we had shared. How could I even consider such a thing when my heart still carried the weight of his absence? How could I let someone else into a space that belonged to him? It wasn't just fear—it was loyalty, pain, and the overwhelming desire to preserve the sanctity of what we had.

But time, as it often does, softened the edges of my grief. It didn't erase it, but it made room for other feelings to emerge. Slowly, hesitantly, I began to heal. My heart, though scarred, started to whisper possibilities I had once silenced. I started to ask myself: Could there be a second chance at life? Could there be a companion who would walk with me, not to replace Shivam, but to walk alongside the love I still carry for him?

Yet, even as these thoughts surfaced, they brought with them a flood of doubts. What if I opened myself up only to face more loss? What if the next chapter of my story brought disappointment, compromise, or a life that felt disconnected from the values I hold dear?

During one of these sleepless nights of reflection, I came across a quote by Immanuel Kant:

"I had to deny knowledge in order to make room for faith."

These words echoed in my mind, resonating in a way I couldn't ignore. They reminded me that life is unpredictable, that certainty isn't a prerequisite for hope. Faith, I realized, isn't about knowing what lies ahead. It's about taking a leap into the unknown, trusting that even in uncertainty, there is the possibility of something beautiful.

With this realization, I found a way to reframe my journey. I wasn't betraying Shivam by opening myself to the idea of remarriage; I was honoring the love we shared. I will forever be thankful to him for teaching me what it feels like to love and be loved so deeply. His love transformed me, gave me strength I didn't know I had, and shaped the person I am today.

I often think of how Shivam used to look at me during our arguments or in moments of quiet pain. He would say, his voice a mix of frustration and tenderness, *"The only thing that makes me weak and frustrated is the pain in your eyes."*

Even now, when the tears come—and they do come—I remind myself of those words. I imagine him watching over me, and I want him to see not just the grief, but the resilience he always believed I had. I want him to look down, smile, and think, *"That's the girl I fell in love with, married, and trusted with our son's life."*

Faith doesn't come easily to someone who has been through loss. It's fragile, hesitant, and sometimes feels foolish. But I've learned that it's also the most courageous thing you can hold onto. It's what allows you to rebuild, to hope, and to keep moving forward—even when the path ahead is unclear.

In choosing to trust life again, I am choosing to honor both Shivam and myself. I am choosing to love myself enough to believe that there is more to my story and that the chapters yet to come can hold joy, connection, and meaning.

Today, I stand at a crossroads, open to remarriage but on my own terms. If I choose to walk down that path, it will be because I've found someone who aligns with my journey, not because society dictates it. If I don't, then I will continue to rise on my own, building a life that is stable, fulfilling, and authentic.

I will not teach my son that love is about compromise without connection. I will not let him grow up believing that a woman's worth is tied to her marital status.

This decision is not rebellion—it is self-awareness. Life's most valuable lessons have taught me to stop seeking validation from the outside and instead build a foundation of inner strength.

To every widow reading this, I ask: Why should our worth be defined by the presence of a man in our lives? Why should our strength be overshadowed by society's discomfort with our independence?

The next time someone tells you to remarry, ask them this: *"What can you do to help me thrive as I am?"*

Let us demand better questions, deeper support, and a broader understanding of what it means to rebuild. Widowhood is not the end of the story—it's an opportunity to rewrite it.

Widowhood is not the end of the story. It's a chance to rewrite it. It's a fire that burns away the illusions, leaving behind a stronger, wiser version of yourself.

I won't sugarcoat it—this journey is painful. But it's also transformative. It teaches you that you are capable of more than you ever imagined. It shows you that love, real love, starts with loving yourself enough to set boundaries, prioritize your peace, and refuse to settle.

The Real Lesson: Patterns and Progress

Life has a way of teaching us the same lessons until we finally learn them. Tarot speaks of this beautifully: the patterns in our lives repeat, not to punish us, but to guide us toward growth.

For me, the lesson was clear. In my younger years, I neglected to build the foundation of self-sufficiency and independence. I let distractions pull me away from creating a secure future, and today, I'm still working to correct those mistakes.

But here's the difference: this time, I'm choosing to face the hard work head-on. My priority is to build a life that is stable, fulfilling, and authentic—not one that simply ticks society's boxes.

Because, I am not incomplete. I am not a project to be fixed. I am a masterpiece in progress—rising, thriving, and proving that even in the face of loss, life can be beautiful.

A Final Reflection Exercise for You

1. **Think about the pressures society has placed on you.**
   - What expectations have you felt forced to meet?
   - How can you create boundaries to protect your mental and emotional health?
2. **Identify the lessons you've been avoiding.**
   - Are there patterns in your life that keep repeating?
   - What steps can you take to finally break free from them?
3. **Write down your dreams and goals.**
   - What do you need to build to create a fulfilling life for yourself?
   - How can you stay true to your values while working toward them?

www.ingramcontent.com/pod-product-compliance
Lightning Source LLC
LaVergne TN
LVHW041209150826
845673LV00001B/339

* 9 7 9 8 8 9 7 2 4 5 4 2 0 *